BEWARE OF THE LEAVEN OF THE PHARISEES

by
David W. Chadwell

QUALITY PUBLICATIONS
P.O. BOX 1060
ABILENE, TEXAS 79604

ISBN: 0-89137-566-X

DEDICATION

To Anita, Kevin, Jon, and Sherri
May you live under the authority of Christ
and in the spirit of His teachings.

TABLE OF CONTENTS

PREFACE

The author presents this book in a spirit of fearfulness. The possible criticism of brothers who defend differing perspectives is not the reason for that fearfulness. The reason for the fearfulness is this: some who read the material will neither recognize nor understand the reality of the problem of modern Pharisaism. It is the fear that those Christians will react to the presentation of the problem instead of prayerfully studying a threatening reality. It is the fear that some will misunderstand because they will examine sections in search of flaws rather than reading the whole to understand the problem.

Two kinds of Christians serve as the focus for these fears. The first are those who unthinkingly have turned Christian existence into ritualistic legalism, but who do not realize what they have done. It will be easy for these Christians to seek to justify themselves instead of examining the inadequacies of this approach to Biblical spirituality. The second are the discouraged, disheartened brethren who see the effects of Scriptureless legalism which some have sought to bind on the church. It will be easy for them in impatience to censure their brethren rather than to seek to build constructive understandings.

The problem this book deals with is not new. It is as old as the restoration movement, as old as the New Testament church. It will exist in every generation of Christians. No single author or select group of brethren within the kingdom will resolve the problem even for his generation. New Testament Christians will struggle with the proper interpretation of Scripture and with the identification of the true spirit of Christ as long as this earth continues.

This book is not the product of a "sudden inspiration." The concern was born years ago when the author began to study New Testament backgrounds. The concern was focused by those studies and by four years of mission work in West Africa. The realities of cross-culture evangelism revealed how much of the American culture has been infused into American concepts of New Testament Christianity. The thesis of the book was formulated over five years prior to the completion of the manuscript. The available time of three years was used to research and to produce the manuscript. Parts of the first manuscript were rewritten five times. When the first completed manuscript was submitted for publication consideration, some scholarly friends made some critical, constructive suggestions. That resulted in additional research and a complete revision of over one-half of the manuscript.

The author pretends to be neither a scholar nor an expert. He is a student with an unending dedication to learning. He acknowledges that just critical evaluations can be made of the material. He is hopeful that the question raised in the book is dealt with from a Biblical perspective which is in complete keeping with the genuine spirit of Christ. He is not pretentious in believing that this material is the solution to a complex problem. He is prayerful that the material makes a positive contribution toward understanding a problem which seems destined once again to becoming a serious brotherhood crisis.

This material is presented in a spirit of concern for the church, in a spirit of love for the brotherhood, and in full faith in the restoration approach to the establishment of first-century Christianity. It is not presented in a spirit of combativeness or hostility. The question is not, "Who loves the truth?" It is not, "Is Scripture the revealed truth of God?" The questions are, "(a) How do we determine the proper meaning of revealed truth? (b) how do we appropriate that meaning in the full spirit of Christ? and (c) how do we use that meaning to produce minds, hearts, and lives of Christ-defined spirituality?"

If in any way this material does not reflect an honest spirit of brotherly love and of respectful concern, the author asks the readers' forgiveness in those matters.

CHAPTER ONE
WHO WERE THESE ANTAGONISTS?

The common Christian stereotype of the Pharisee is "the hypocritical enemy of Jesus." The basis for that stereotype is the fact that the gospels frequently present the Pharisees in the role of Jesus' antagonists. Early in Jesus' ministry, they became His opponents. They grew increasingly hostile as His popularity and influence grew among the Jewish populace.

Matthew's first reference to the Pharisees records John the Baptizer castigating the Pharisees and Sadducees who visited him in the desert as "offspring of vipers."[1] Matthew also records numerous antagonistic encounters between Jesus and the Pharisees. The Pharisees criticized Jesus for eating with tax collectors and sinners.[2] They claimed His power to heal came from the prince of demons.[3] One Sabbath as they followed Jesus, they accused His disciples of violating the Sabbath when they stripped ripened grain from stalks along the path.[4] They conferred among themselves seeking a way to destroy Him.[5] They asked Him for a sign which would prove His relationship with God.[6] They asked why His disciples did not keep the authoritative traditional teachings.[7] By using a controversial divorce question, they tried to trap Him in His teachings.[8] They wanted to arrest Him.[9] They sent people to "respectfully" ask Him a trick question concerning taxes in a deliberate plan to "ensnare" Him in His teachings.[10]

Mark records several of the same incidents: the criticism of Jesus for eating and drinking with sinners and tax collectors,[11] the criticism of the disciples for stripping grain on the Sabbath,[12] their being offended by Jesus' healing on the Sabbath,[13] the criticism of the disciples for violating the tradition of the elders,[14] their asking for a sign,[15] the

7

attempt to trap Him with the divorce question,[16] and the attempt to trap Him with the question about taxes.[17] Early in the gospel, Mark notes that the Pharisees and Herodians were conspiring in seeking a way to destroy Jesus.[18]

Luke also notes the Pharisees' reactions to Jesus' eating with tax collectors and sinners[19] and to the disciples' stripping grain on the Sabbath.[20] However, Luke adds considerable additional information about their antagonistic feelings. When Jesus forgave the palsied man of his sins, the Pharisees began "reasoning" that Jesus had blasphemed.[21] Early Luke notes that the Pharisees and doctors of the law from every village of Galilee and Judea and from Jerusalem assembled to hear Jesus' teachings.[22] After Jesus' indictment of the Pharisees and lawyers, the scribes and Pharisees "began to press upon him vehemently and to provoke him to say many things; laying wait for him, to catch something out of his mouth."[23] Once they tried to frighten Him away from Jerusalem by warning Him that Herod Antipas wished to kill Him.[24] After His teaching on materialism, they scoffed at Him.[25]

Luke also documents occasions of association between Jesus and the Pharisees. Simon, a Pharisee, invited Jesus to eat with him, and Jesus accepted.[26] Jesus accepted another Pharisee's invitation to breakfast.[27] On this occasion Jesus shocked him by not ceremonially washing His hands before eating. On another occasion He ate with one of the rulers of the Pharisees on a Sabbath, and "they" watched Him.[28]

John's material on the Pharisees is unique. He records the respectful visit of Nicodemus, a Pharisee and a member of the Sanhedrin of seventy-one in Jerusalem.[29] After hearing a Jerusalem multitude's reaction to Jesus' teachings, the chief priests and Pharisees sent officers with instructions to arrest Jesus.[30] The Pharisees and scribes sought to discredit Jesus by bringing Him a woman taken in the act of adultery and demanding that Jesus decide her fate.[31] The Pharisees denounced Jesus as a "man not from God" because He healed a blind man on the Sabbath.[32] This incident reveals the depth of their animosity. The chief priests and Pharisees convened a council of desperation after the resurrection of Lazarus. They saw no effective way to counter Jesus' swelling influence.[33] Later they ordered anyone knowing His whereabouts to reveal it that they might arrest Him.[34] In a further attempt to discourage those who would follow Jesus, the Pharisees declared anyone professing faith in Him would be banned from the synagogue.[35] The arresting officers who accompanied Judas were provided by the chief priests and Pharisees.[36]

The gospels clearly present the Pharisees as formidable antagonists of Jesus.

Not the Sole Antagonists

For much of this century there has been a growing, prominent voice of support for the Pharisees. Some prominent elements of Jewish scholarship and of Protestant scholarship have rejected the gospels' testimony regarding the Pharisees. Elements of Jewish scholarship which seek to heal the breach between Judaism and Christianity do so by defending the Pharisees. Elements of Protestant scholarship use higher criticism to reject the gospels' caricature of the Pharisees. Some of these scholars strongly suggest that the Pharisees were major, helpful contributors to Jesus' ministry. Much of the supportive material favoring the Pharisees implies that Scripture portrays the Pharisees as the only antagonists of Jesus. However, the gospels clearly portray other segments of Jewish society as being equally hostile toward Jesus and His teachings. Among the other antagonists were the chief priests, the scribes, the Jewish elders, the Sadducees, the Herodians, and the lawyers. It must be understood that there would be some overlapping among those groups. Many of the chief priests may have been Sadducees also; many of the scribes also may have been Sadducees or Pharisees; and such would be the case with the elders and the lawyers.

An analysis of each gospel's portrayal of Jesus' antagonists highlights a significant fact. Matthew presents the Pharisees in the role of Jesus' critics and opponents twelve times.[37] Matthew also mentions the chief priests in that role twelve times,[38] the elders ten times,[39] the scribes four times,[40] the Sadducees three times,[41] and the Herodians once.[42]

Mark mentions the Pharisees as opponents and critics seven times.[43] Mark also mentions the chief priests in that role twelve times,[44] the scribes seven times,[45] the elders three times,[46] the Herodians twice,[47] and the Sadducees once.[48]

Luke places the Pharisees in the role of Jesus' critics and opponents twelve times.[49] The chief priests are placed in that role ten times,[50] the scribes seven times,[51] the lawyers four times,[52] the elders twice,[53] and the Sadducees once.[54]

John places the Pharisees in that role nine times.[55] The chief priests are placed in that role seven times,[56] and the scribes once.[57]

It is abundantly obvious that the gospels do not present the Pharisees as the only antagonists of Jesus. There were many Jewish antagonists of Jesus.

Who Were the Pharisees?

The origin of the Pharisees is a subject of considerable disagreement. There are numerous views in regard to the inception and the development of Pharisaism, and several of these views are in significant disagreement. There are two basic reasons for such conflicting views. Reason one: there is a meager amount of specific, factual information to be used to trace their origin and development. A small amount of information is subject to many interpretations. Reason two: there is a significant degree of difficulty in determining the appropriate way to interpret correctly the cultural and religious background and perspective of intertestamental and first-century writings.

There is even uncertainty in regard to the meaning of the name, Pharisee. Several positions are held in regard to the origin of the word. View one: the word denotes Jews who preserved their purity by being* separatists.[58] View two: the name evolved from root words meaning "expounder" or "interpreter," denoting the role of the Pharisee as a teacher of the Torah.[59] The Torah or Law was the books of Genesis through Deuteronomy. View three: originally, the name was a derisive term given to the Hasidim by their enemies.[60] In time it became a respectable name. There are additional variations of each of these views.

The most common view held concerning their origin declares that the Pharisees evolved in some manner from the spirit or the activities of the Hasidim of the intertestamental period. The Hasidim or "pious ones" regarded themselves as being the orthodox Jew. They held strict religious views based on the Mosaical covenant, and they maintained a zealous commitment to ancient Judaism and its ways. Political and national aspirations were of little interest. They were devoted to preserving the old paths against cultural changes and a changing world.

The Basic Concern

While there is much yet to be resolved about the origin of Pharisaism, there is broad agreement concerning the basic concern of Pharisaism. A dire threat to the survival of Judaism began with the Babylonian captivity (597 BC). From its beginnings, Judaism was designed to be a national religion of a settled, localized people. They would have one center of sacrificial worship.[61] Attendance to national religious festivals would be within ability of all and compulsory for all the men.[62] A priesthood would be accessible to the populace and capable of meeting their religious needs.

The Babylonian captivity created a dilemma with which Judaism was not designed to cope. That dilemma threatened to destroy the Jewish people as a distinctive society and Judaism as a religion. The temple was in ruins and its site far away. Sacrificial worship as originally instituted was impossible. With no temple in which to serve, the priests could not function in their ancient role. Religious festivals and pilgrimages as they had been observed in Palestine were impossible. The threat of assimilation was a deadly problem. How could the Jews prevent their being assimilated into the Babylonian culture? How could they in exile preserve their distinctiveness religiously and nationally?

Judaism's survival of the Babylonian captivity and the return of some to Palestine did not end the threat. After being permitted to return to their land, they were still under the control and influence of the Persians. They were to remain a subjugated people for generations following the return as they were controlled by the Egyptians, subjugated by the Greeks under Alexander the Great, and ruled by the Syrians.

The most serious threat came from the Syrian determination to eradicate Jewish culture and religion and to replace it with the Greek culture. Antiochus IV Epiphanes made a cruel, determined effort to destroy Judaism.[63] His repressive measures included execution of those possessing Scripture and of mothers with circumcized infants and their infants. This attempt to Hellenize Jewish society was welcomed by some Jews. They preferred acceptance of a "modern" culture and entrance into the mainstream of the "modern" world. They detested the rest of the nation's attempt to maintain religious and cultural isolation.

Beginning with the Babylonian captivity and continuing through much of the intertestamental period, the survival of Judaism was continually threatened. Those periods thrust Judaism into uncontrollable contact with pagan societies and subjected it to the demands and stresses of the changing world. When Judaism existed primarily as an isolationist society and religion, the society and the religion could be regulated by the Mosaical covenant with reasonable ease. In isolation and a semi-controlled society the Torah could always contain "the answer." Most of religious and social needs were generated by the role of the Torah as the foundation of religion and culture.

However, beginning with the Babylonian captivity, the Jews were dominated by the Babylonians, the Persians, the Egyptians, the Greeks, and the Syrians. Such dominations ended convenient isolation and forced interaction with other cultures and religions. The end result was new social circumstances, new religious questions about life and existence, new ways of living, new moral dilemmas, new ethical questions, new aspects of human needs, and differing religious demands. Frequently the Torah did not specifically address these new questions, thoughts, and situations. There was a growing demand that Judaism and the Torah provide meaningful, effective answers for these new questions, thoughts, and situations created by interaction with the changing world and pagan cultures.

As has always been typical of most religous movements, Judaism had formulated, maintained, and defended "pat answers" which had served as the authoritative position in regard to most religious matters. Those "pat answers" were sufficient as long as the society was isolated and the real needs of daily life situations remained basically unchanged. However, when isolation ended, when the real needs of daily life situations changed through contact with differing cultures, and when social change produced new moral/ethical dilemmas, many of the "pat answers" became irrelevant, meaningless, and ineffective.

At some point in this period, Pharisaism evolved. It derived its impetus from two basic concerns. The first concern was the desire to preserve and to maintain Judaism's old paths and ancient ways. If the ancient ways were to survive, Judaism had to answer effectively the new moral/ethical questions and to meet the real needs of the daily life situation. Ineffective, irrelevant "pat answers" from a world and society which no longer existed would have doomed Judaism to becoming a dead religion. Teachings of the Torah had to harmonize with the realities of the existing world.

The second concern was the desire to answer the questions and issues of the day by making the spirit and the intent of the Torah relevant to the problems and needs of daily life. The true spirit of the Torah and God's intent in the Torah had to be applicable to all life's realities in that present age.

Pharisaism did not evolve and never existed as an attempt to by-pass or to minimize the teachings of the Torah. It came into being and existed as a determined effort to preserve fully the teachings of the Torah.

CHAPTER ONE
FOOTNOTES

1. *Matthew 3:7.*
2. *Matthew 9:11.*

3. *Matthew 9:34; 12:24.*

4. *Matthew 12:2.*

5. *Matthew 12:14.*

6. *Matthew 12:34; 16:1.*

7. *Matthew 15:1-2.*

8. *Matthew 19:3-4.*

9. *Matthew 21:45-46.*

10. *Matthew 22:15*

11. *Mark 2:16.*

12. *Mark 2:24.*

13. *Mark 3:6*

14. *Mark 7:1-5.*

15. *Mark 8:11.*

16. *Mark 10:2.*

17. *Mark 12:13.*

18. *Mark 3:6.*

19. *Luke 5:30; 15:1-2.*

20. *Luke 6:2.*

21. *Luke 5:21; Mark notes that the scribes made that criticism, Mark 2:6-7.*

22. *Luke 5:17.*

23. *Luke 11:53-54.*

24. *Luke 13:31.*

25. *Luke 16:14.*

26. *Luke 7:36*

27. *Luke 11:37-38.*

28. *Luke 14:1.*

29. *John 3:1-15.*

30. *John 7:32.*

31. *John 8:3.*

32. *John 9:13-34.*

33. *John 11:47-48.*

34. *John 11:57.*

35. *John 12:42.*

36. *John 18:3.*

37. *Matthew 9:11; 9:34; 12:2,14; 12:24; 12:38; 15:1; 16:1; 19:3; 21:45-46; 22:15; 22:34-35; 27:62-63.*

38. *Matthew 16:21; 20:18; 21:23; 21:15; 21:45; 26:3-4; 26:47; 26:59; 27:1; 27:12; 27:20; 27:41.*

39. *Matthew 16:21; 21:23; 26:3-4; 26:14; 26:47; 26:49; 27:1; 27:12; 27:20, 27:41.*

40. *Matthew 20:19; 21:15; 27:41; 15:1.*

41. *Matthew 16:1; 16:6, 12; 22:23.*

42. *Matthew 22:16.*

43. *Mark 2:16; 2:24; 3:6; 7:1-5; 8:11; 10:2; 12:13.*

44. *Mark 8:31; 10:33; 11:18; 11:27; 14:1; 14:10-11; 14:43; 14:55; 15:1; 15:3; 15:10-11; 15:31.*

45. *Mark 8:31; 10:33; 11:18; 11:27; 14:1; 14:43; 15:31.*

46. *Mark 8:31; 11:27; 14:48.*

47. *Mark 3:6; 12:13.*

48. *Mark 12:18.*

49. *Luke 5:21; 5:30; 6:2; 6:7; 7:30; 7:39; 11:53; 13:31; 15:2; 16:14; 17:20; 19:39.*

50. *Luke 9:22; 19:47; 20:1; 20:19; 20:22; 22:4; 22:66; 23:10; 23:13; 24:10.*

51. *Luke 9:22; 19:47; 20:1; 20:19; 20:22; 22:66; 23:10.*

52. *Luke 5:17; 10:25; 11:45-52; 14:3.*

53. *Luke 9:22; 20:1.*

54. *Luke 20:27.*

55. *John 7:32, 47; 8:3-5; 8:13; 9:16; 11:47; 11:57; 12:19; 12:42; 18:3.*

56. *John 7:32; 11:47; 11:57; 12:10-11; 18:3; 18:35; 19:6.*

57. *John 8:3.*

58. D. S. Russell, **The Jews from Alexander to Herod** *(London: Oxford University Press, 1967), pp. 162-163.*

59. *Samuel Sandmel,* **Judaism and Christian Beginnings** *(New York: Oxford University Press, 1978), p. 159.*

60. *Louis Finkelstein,* **Pharisaism In The Making** *(KTAY Publishing House, Inc., 1972), p. 187, note 1.*

61. *Deuteronomy 12:5-14.*

62. *Exodus 23:17; Deuteronomy 16:16-17.*

63. *Josephus,* **Antiquities of the Jews,** *12.5.4.*

CHAPTER ONE
QUESTIONS

1. What is the common Christian stereotype of the Pharisees?

2. List some of the information given about the Pharisees in Matthew, Mark, and Luke.

3. What does Luke record about Jesus and the Pharisees in Luke 7:36-50, 11:37-41, and 14:1-6?

4. Give the unique information about the Pharisees found in the gospel of John.

5. List Jesus' other antagonists. Identify each group.

6. Why are there many views held about the origin of the Pharisees?

7. What is the Torah?

8. What is the most common view held about the origin of the Pharisees?

9. How did the Babylonian captivity threaten the survival of Judaism?

10. Explain how both exile and domination by pagan societies affected Judaism for generations following the Babylonian captivity.

11. Give the two basic concerns of the Pharisaic movement as it evolved.

12. What was the objective of Pharisiasm in regard to the Torah?

THOUGHT QUESTION

Why do people always desire "pat answers" to religious questions? Why are all "pat answers" destined to become irrelevant and ineffective?

CHAPTER TWO
A CLEARER PERSPECTIVE

The traditional views commonly held by most Christians in regard to the Pharisees are often inaccurate over-simplifications or erroneous ideas. Those views often form a stereotyped concept of the Pharisees which results in two unfortunate problems. First, the stereotype is an injustice to the Pharisees which generates a misunderstanding of them. Second, the stereotype causes today's Christian to miss the point of Jesus' teachings concerning the Pharisees. Unquestionably, Christians need a clearer perspective of the Pharisees and Pharisaism.

The Brotherhood of Pharisees

The Pharisees as a sect were highly organized. They were a community, a brotherhood with rules, officers, regular meeting times, and procedures for admitting new members and disciplining old members.[1] They came primarily from middle class urban Jewish society: shopkeepers and skilled artisans.[2] As a compact, disciplined body, they were characterized by unshakable conviction and unyielding determination.[3]

A society of the Pharisees was known as a *chabura,* and laymen members were *chaberim.*[4] A true *chaber* (member) accepted the duty of ritual cleanness and the obligation to pay the temple tax.[5] A member guilty of transgressions was expelled, but he could be readmitted.[6] The society maintained basic statutes which regulated the lives of members and which regulated admissions and expulsions.[7] A candidate for admission to the society had to pass a period of testing.[8] A major objective of the society was to incorporate the priestly law into everyday life.[9] Members restricted themselves to the dietary laws of purity.[10]

Pharisaic societies existed in small groups.[11] Though the Pharisees were relatively small in numbers, the organization of their brotherhood gave them an influence on Judaism out of proportion to their size.[12]

A Multifaceted Sect

The misconception concerning the Pharisees is that all Pharisees held the same views, positions, and concepts in common as a religious sect. In the first century they enjoyed the greatest popularity of the religious sects among the common people.[13] However, like any significant religious group, Pharisaism encompassed sub-groups who were in agreement on basic issues and views, but also were in disagreement over many issues. What was characteristic of Pharisees in general might not be characteristic of certain groups or certain individuals within Pharisaism.

New Testament notations verify that all Pharisees were not alike in their religious views. The Pharisee Nicodemus approached Jesus with genuine respect noting that Jesus was a teacher sent from God.[14] On another occasion he sought a fair hearing for Jesus.[15] At Jesus' death, he bought a hundred pounds of spices to be used in Jesus' burial.[16] The prominent Pharisee Gamaliel influenced the Sanhedrin not to kill the apostles by declaring,"Refrain from these men, and let them alone; for if this counsel of this work be of men, it will be overthrown: but if it is of God, ye will not be able to overthrow them; lest haply ye be found even to be fighting against God."[17] Saul, or Paul, was a Pharisee prior to conversion.[18] As a Pharisee he was a violent man with little compassion for people.[19] However, he was aboltely genuine at all times in his religious convictions and deeds. He could say with complete honesty that he always had lived in complete accord with his conscience.[20] That he was devout, sincere, committed, and totally consumed in the fervor of his convictions is an established fact.

The *Talmud* clearly acknowledges there were many types of Pharisees. It divides Pharisees into seven catagories: the "shoulder" *(skikmi)* Pharisee; the "delaying" *(nikpi)* Pharisee; the "bruised" *(kizai)* Pharisee; the "pestle" Pharisee; the "what is my duty" Pharisee; the "from love of God" Pharisee; and the "from fear of God" Pharisee.[21]

The "shoulder" Pharisee ostentatiously acted on unworthy motives parading his religious duties on his shoulders. The "delaying" Pharisee asked people to wait while he did a good deed. The "bruised" Pharisee walked into walls as he tried to avoid looking at women. The "pestle" Pharisee with a false sense of humility walked with his head bowed down like a pestle in a mortar. The "what is my duty" Pharisee asked that question to get others to extol his virtue.[22] The admirable Pharisee was the one who like Abraham loved God.[23]

The extent of fragmentation within Pharisaism is strikingly evident from another perspective. There were at least four major sects of the Jews in the first century prior to the Roman-Jewish war: the Pharisees, the Sadducees, the Zealots, and the Essenes. The sect of the Zealots established by Judas the Galilean was devoted to Jewish independence and "agree(d) in all other things with the Pharisees."[24] Their primary distinction from the Pharisees was their radical devotion to nationalism.[25] The Essenes were isolationists who lived in communes in a determined effort to separate themselves from decadent Judaism.[26] Some scholars identify them as a branch of Pharisaism.[27] The Zealots and the Essenes can be regarded as radical factions of Pharisaism.

Within the mainstream of Pharisaism there were open, rivaling, divergent religious views and positions. At times there were grave divisions produced by disagreements over the correct interpretation of the law. The first-century leaders of the Pharisees, Hillel and Shammai, were in particular conflict.[28] Shammai favored severe penalties for any infringement of the law and strict adherence to its harsh demands. Hillel was devoted to peace with a conviction that the law must deal with problems humanely. These two schools were in constant disagreement throughout most of the first century.[29]

To view all Pharisees as being identical in attitude and in religious views is a serious misconception.

Pharisaic Hypocrisy

The charge Jesus made against the Pharisees which is best remembered is the charge of hypocrisy. That charge is made only five times: Matthew 15:7; 22:18; 23:13, 15, 23, 27, 29 (one discourse); Mark 7:6; and Luke 12:1. In addition to this charge, he also charged them with the following: having inadequate righteousness,[30] being an "evil and adulterous generation,"[31] having harmful influence in their teaching,[32] loving money,[33] and being egotistically self-righteous.[34]

An analysis of Matthew 23, the extensive charge of Pharisaic hypocrisy, is revealing. Their hypocrisy arose from the following attitudes and actions:

1. They bound burdens on others they refused to accept.[35]

2. Their controlling motivation was the hunger for praise and honor.[36]

19

3. They deliberately prohibited people from entering the kingdom.[37]

4. Because of their influence their converts were two-fold more sons of hell.[38]

5. They made artificial, meaningless religious distinctions.[39]

6. Their concern for minutia obscured matters of grave importance.[40]

7. They were concerned about the appearance of purity, not about being pure.[41]

8. They honored the prophets while holding the attitudes of those who had killed the prophets.[42]

Please note Jesus' charges were based on the religious influence of their lives, their personal spiritual motivations, their religious attitudes, and their misrepresentation of the intent of Scripture.

It is obvious that Jesus' concept of hypocrisy and today's common concept of hypocrisy are two different concepts. Today, a hypocrite is a shallow, insincere person who consciously and knowingly is dedicated to deceiving other people about his spiritual commitment. He deliberately creates and wears a false religious front. He knows he is a hypocrite. Rarely will one see any Christian regard another religious person as being hypocritical if that person is obviously sincere in his convictions. Such a person may be accused of being wrong, mistaken, or in error, but not of hypocrisy.

The Root of Pharisaic Hypocrisy

The Pharisees did not regard themselves as being hypocrites. As far as they were concerned, they sincerely lived by their convictions. As an example, consider the Pharisee's prayer in Luke 18:11-12. The fault with his prayer did not lie in his declarations being false. No doubt he was not an extortioner, unjust (by his definition), or an adulterer. Doubtlessly he did fast twice a week and give tithes of all he had (probably including mint, anise, and cummin). It is probable that Christians of today would not have called the Pharisees of the first century hypocrites.

The hypocrisy of the Pharisees did not lie in consciously deceitful lives, or in a shallow, insincere pretense of religious commitment. From today's perspective on hypocrisy, they were not conscious, willful hypocrites deceiving everyone around them. The source of their hypocrisy is much more fearful and sobering. They were hypocrites as a result of holding and defending distorted perspectives and perverted values.

Consider some expressions of Pharisaic hypocrisy. Saul could be committed devoutly to the law of God, and at the same time without a bad conscience he would commit fellow Jews to death if they followed Christ. Vicious hatred and godliness are hardly compatible companions. The Pharisees could stress the importance of the ten commandments and yet violate them for what they regarded as being honorable religious reasons. In seeking to apply scriptural principle to current life, they rationalized away the basic intent of Scripture. In Matthew 15:1-9 Jesus demonstrated this fact. A person could by authoritative, accepted religious principle willfully refuse to honor his father and mother. For a religious reason he could reject one of the ten commandments. The Pharisees stringently endorsed the law, "Thou shalt not kill."[43] Yet, when Jesus' influence soared following the resurrection of Lazarus, they in good conscience could decide to put Jesus to death with this justification: ". . . it is expedient for you that one man should die for the people, and that the whole nation perish not."[44] They would demand obedience to the law, "thou shalt not bear false witness against thy neighbor."[45] Yet, since they were convinced that Jesus was a false teacher and a grave threat religiously to Israel, they could seek and tolerate false witnesses at Jesus' trial as they searched for some pretext on which to execute him.[46] In their thinking, "valid" religious concerns or serious religious "crises" provided justification for violation of basic divine commandments. It was in keeping with divine will and law to violate divine will and law. Such perverted understandings make a sham of divine teaching and constitute the ultimate expression of hypocrisy.

The Fearfulness of Pharisaic Hypocrisy

This truest form of hypocrisy is as much alive among Christians today as it was among the Pharisees. Were Jesus to visit His church today, there would be committed people He would declare to be hypocrites for the same reasons which He used to indict the Pharisees. For example, the teachings of the New Testament concerning Christian unity and mutual Christian love are clear, specific, and undeniable.[47] John stated the importance of these divine expectations quite simply: "He that loveth not abideth in death. Whosoever hateth his brother is a murderer: and ye know no murderer hath eternal life abiding in him."[48]

Yet, committed Christians dedicated to the authority of Scripture find every form of religious justification for despising, branding, and vindictively fighting other equally committed baptized believers with

21

whom they disagree. Public accusations are caustically hurled. Biting indictments are printed and circulated. Waves of "confidential" material are communicated orally resulting in gossip and distorted half-truths. In such circumstances there is no brotherly respect, let alone brotherly love. Passages such as Romans 14 are completely ignored. Thus, factions of baptized believers all seeking to be the Lord's true church, each convicted and sincerely determined to defend "the faith," seek to destroy or to devour each other over matters of judgment. All factions completely ignore the ethic of *agape* love[49] and the divine injunction to be one in Christ as He and the Father are one.[50]

In the midst of such internal warring and hatreds, the same factions preach to a denominational world the absolute necessity for the unity of believers and a brotherhood of love using the very passages which they are disregarding. As the message falls on deaf ears, they wonder aloud why the religious world cannot capture the vision of simple unity on the basis of the authority of Scripture. Never do they see the inconsistency of their own hypocrisy.

Pharisaical hypocrisy is quite alive today.

CHAPTER TWO
FOOTNOTES

1. *T. W. Manson,* **The Servant Messiah** *(Grand Rapids: Baker Book House, 1977), p. 22.*

2. *Ibid.*

3. *Ibid.*

4. *Gerhard Kittel and Gerhard Friedrich, eds., "pharisaios,"* **Theological Dictionary of the New Testament,** *9 vols., trans. Geoffrey W. Bromiley (Grand Rapids: Wm. B. Eerdmans Publishing Co., 1974), 9:17.*

5. *Ibid., p. 18.*

6. *Ibid.*

7. *Ibid.*

8. *Ibid.*

9. *Ibid., p. 19.*

10. *Ibid., p. 20.*

11. *Ibid., p. 19*

12. *Russell, p. 161.*
13. *Josephus,* **Antiquities of the Jews,** *13.10.6.*
14. *John 3:1-2.*
15. *John 7:50-51.*
16. *John 19:39.*
17. *Acts 5:34, 38-39.*
18. Acts 26:5; Philippians 3:5.
19. *Acts 26:10-11; 1 Timothy 1:13.*
20. *Acts 23:1; 24:16; 2 Timothy 1:3.*
21. *T. B. Sotah 22b.*
22. *Ibid.*
23. *Sandmel, p. 161.*
24. *Josephus,* **Antiquities of the Jews,** *18.1.6.*
25. *Ibid.*
26. *Ibid., 18.1.5.*
27. **Encyclopedia Judaica,** *Vol. 6, "Essenes," p. 800.*
28. *W. D. Davies,* **Introduction To Pharisaism** *(Philadelphia: Fortress Press, 1967), p. 17.*
29. *Ibid., p. 18.*
30. *Matthew 5:20.*
31. *Matthew 12:39.*
32. *Matthew 16:6, 12.*
33. *Luke 16:14.*
34. *Luke 18:10-12.*
35. *Matthew 23:4.*
36. *Matthew 23:5-7.*
37. *Matthew 23:13.*
38. *Matthew 23:15.*
39. *Matthew 23:16-22.*
40. *Matthew 23:23-24.*
41. *Matthew 23:25-28.*
42. *Matthew 23:29-36.*

43. *Exodus 20:13.*

44. *John 11:50.*

45. *Exodus 20:16.*

46. *Matthew 26:59-62.*

47. *John 17:20-21; 1 Corinthians 1:10; John 15:12; 1 Corinthians 13.*

48. *1 John 3:15b-16.*

49. *John 13:34-35.*

50. *John 17:21.*

CHAPTER TWO
QUESTIONS

1. Why is the traditional stereotyped view of the Pharisees an unfortunate view?

2. Discuss the Pharisees as a sect or society.

3. How do the following factors demonstrate that all Pharisees did not hold the same views in regard to all issues and concepts:
   A. Nicodemus, Gamaliel, and Paul
   B. The *Talmud's* classifications
   C. The Zealots and Essenes
   D. Hillel and Shammai

4. What was the basis of Jesus' charge that the Pharisees were hypocrites?

5. Contrast today's concept of hypocrisy and Jesus' concept of hypocrisy.

6. Did the Pharisees regard themselves as being hypocrites? Explain your answer.

7. Use the following to illustrate Pharisaic hypocrisy.
   A. Saul (Paul) before conversion
   B. Matthew 15:1-9
   C. Exodus 20:13 with John 11:50
   D. Exodus 20:16 with Matthew 26:49-62.

8. What is the ultimate expression of hypocrisy?

9. On what basis could Jesus condemn some committed Christians in His church today for Pharisaic hypocrisy?

THOUGHT QUESTION

Using Jesus' definition of hypocrisy, what kind of Christians in the church today would be hypocrites? Would they know they were hypocrites? Why?

CHAPTER THREE

THE TRADITION OF THE FATHERS

The core of numerous Pharisaic indictments against Jesus was the implied or declared accusation that he transgressed the tradition of the elders.[1] This accusation which indicted Jesus for rejecting or for violating proper authority lies at the foundation of all religious discussions and decisions. If a person is to make proper spiritual determinations and to base his religious life on spiritual truth, his actions and knowledge must be rooted in proper authority.

Determining proper spiritual authority is an ancient but continuing problem. Declaring Scripture as authority does not resolve the problem. One can accept Scripture as authority, but be unable to determine the true meaning of Scripture. One can advocate Scripture as authority but be unable to apply the meaning of Scripture to daily life and conduct. One can advocate Scripture as authority but believe and abide by principles which Scripture never teaches. In any one of these instances, accepting Scripture as authority does not result in living by the authority of Scripture.

The Question of Authority

The Pharisees and Sadducees were in frequent disagreement over the question of religious authority. Both accepted the Torah as authoritative, as did all Jewish sects. However, they were in frequent disagreement over the application of the Torah to current life situations and needs.

First-century Judaism's circumstances had changed drastically from the circumstances of pre-exilic Judaism. As an example, one of the results of the Babylonian captivity was the *diaspora*. From the Babylonian captivity forward, more Jews lived outside Palestine than within Palestine. These devout Jews living in other countries were the *diaspora* (the dispersed ones). In the first century, colonies of the Jews lived all over the civilized world.

The religious needs and circumstances of *diaspora* Jews totally differed from those of Palestinian Jews. For many of the *diaspora*, pilgrimages to attend the religious feasts at Jerusalem were impossible. The temple was unavailable to them for sacrificial worship. Living in the midst of Gentile populations radically altered their social circumstances. How did the *diaspora* determine what was correct religiously when the Torah did not address their particular situation? When the Torah was silent about a religious issue or moral question, how could one authoritatively determine what was religiously proper?

The Pharisees addressed this critical problem in these ways. First, they regarded the writings[2] and the prophets[3] as commentaries on and interpretations of the meaning, the intent, and the spirit of the Torah.[4] They stressed that understanding the meaning of the Torah was more important than going by the letter of the Torah.

Second, they addressed questions and needs produced by the changing world by accepting the tradition of the fathers, the oral law, as a source of religious authority. To the Pharisee there were two valid sources of authority: the written Scripture and the oral law.[5] Both were of equal value. Both were of equal authority.[6] The oral law was not to be in contradiction to the written law. Should such a contradiction occur, the written law took precedent.

The Concept of Tradition

Few Christians today understand what the Pharisees called tradition. The religious meaning of the word today has little in common with its meaning to the Pharisees. The Pharisees maintained the law was given in two forms at Sinai: the written form recorded by Moses and an oral, unwritten form. Just as the written form had been preserved by the careful work of scribes, the oral form had been preserved by faithful men who passed it from generation to generation.[7] This claim of antiquity for the oral law was at best a "half-conscious" fiction.[8]

The Pharisees held a specific view of the Torah. They believed God intended through the Torah to regulate every aspect of life. The Torah contained the wisdom of God which was capable of such regulation. Regardless of cost, the Torah was to be preserved. However, for the Torah to regulate all of life, it could be and must be interpreted.[9] Judaism was a living religion capable of being adapted to man's diverse, changing needs.[10] The oral law was the interpretation of the written law making it applicable to the current religious questions and needs.

The oral law or tradition was not a collection of mindless habits or rituals which were honored merely because they were old. It was an elaborate system of religious principles and regulations designed to give an individual practical religious guidance in every aspect of life.[11] The oral law provided an answer when a person wondered, "What should I do in this situation? How do I properly comply with the law in this matter? What is the correct thing to do in fulfilling religious responsibility in this circumstance?" Tradition interpreted revelation: the unwritten law defined how the written law was to be carried out and enforced in virtually every situation.[12] The oral law was always more comprehensive, more extensive than the written law because the oral law grew out of the needs of the times and changed with the times.[13] The oral law served two basic roles: (1) it interpreted and applied the written law; (2) it supplemented the written law.[14] This approach to determining religious conduct was known as Mishnah law.[15] Authoritative religious regulations could be given independent of written Scripture without written Scripture as its source.

These traditional laws did not come into existence by a group of scribes or rabbis gathering and arbitrarily composing them. Neither did they come into existence by scribes and rabbis disregarding written Scripture. The object was not to bypass written Scripture, but to make written Scripture understandable and obeyable. Tradition came into existence because of the love and reverence for written Scripture. The Pharisee believed tradition and the Torah came from the same source for the same purpose; the two could not be separated.[16]

The Nature of Oral Law

The Pharisees approached written Scripture with profound reverence and respect. Their objective through the use of the tradition of the fathers was to "build a fence around the law."[17] The extensive system of regulations produced by tradition was to prohibit a person from violating written Scripture. The regulations served as barriers between the person's conduct and violation of the Torah. Breaking a regulation warned one that conduct infringed on dangerous ground. Thus these regulations guaranteed observance of the Torah and defended against violation of the Torah by declaring what one must or must not do in all situations. The first objective of the Pharisee was to preserve the written law through the use of the oral law.

Second, the Levitical code was followed literally, to the letter, in the minutest consideration.[18] Ritual purity was rigidly enforced and maintained. This was the issue when they questioned Jesus about His disciples eating with unwashed hands.[19] The dietary laws were strictly observed. The written law specified what foods were clean and suitable for eating, and those which were unclean and prohibited.[20] These regulations were observed without exception. Tithing, commanded in the written law, was scrupulously observed and enforced.[21] Jesus acknowledged they went so far as to tithe the garden herbs they grew, and He acknowledged such was proper.[22]

The traditions which existed to preserve the Torah were based on long-established customs or principles known as "decrees" *(gezerot)* and "enactments" *(takkanot).*[23] Custom was the accepted and long-established means of fulfilling a written law. For example, the Torah required a written bill of divorce be given a woman at the time of divorce.[24] However, what the bill of divorce was to declare and how it was to be given was not stated in the Torah. Custom determined the nature of the bill and how it was to be given to the woman by virtue of long-established practice. It thereby fulfilled the intent of the written law and became traditional law. Custom served the same function in regard to many other commands in the Torah: how religious taxes were to be paid, how offerings were to be made, and how the holy days were to be observed. The Torah declared these things were to be done. Custom was the manner in which such things had been observed or performed for generations. Thus custom became traditional law.

Enactments which became traditional laws were rabbinical decrees. The objective of such decrees was to rectify a situation wherein the effect of a law was in opposition to the intent of that law.[25] For example, Deuteronomy 15:1-3 declared that loans were to be canceled every seven years. One objective of this law was periodically to free the people from heavy indebtedness thereby enabling them to gain further financial assistance. However, because of the law, moneylenders simply refused to make loans the fifth and sixth years. If it was unlikely that a loan could be repaid before the seventh year, they would not lend the money. In this situation, the effect of the law in actual practice was in opposition to one of the intents of the law. In this matter an enactment declared that a proper court document sealed by judges or witnesses provided the lender the right to reclaim his loan at any time.[26] Lenders thus protected were willing to make loans in the fifth and sixth years.

The Flaw

It is obvious that the intent of oral law (the traditions of the fathers) was to preserve the spirit, meaning, and authority of the written law, not to set the written law aside. As often is the case, the intent and the effect can be in direct opposition. One of Jesus' objections to the Pharisees' application of the traditional law was its effect. At times it had the effect of nullifying or setting aside a written commandment.[27]

Because the oral law sought to define proper conduct in all situations, it became a rigid form of legalism, an endless collection of rules and regulations to be kept. This legalism became formalism. Thought and understanding were not essential. Compliance with the regulations was essential. One could go through all the forms of complying with the rules and regulations with little personal feeling for God or little understanding. Compliance easily could be substituted for love for God and for faith based on understanding.

It was this flaw that frequently brought Jesus and the Pharisees into conflict. In seeking to preserve the law, traditions at times obscured the law. In seeking to declare the intent of the law, traditions at times violated the law. In seeking to honor the law, traditions at times erased the law by building faith in rules and regulations rather than in God and His Word.

CHAPTER THREE
FOOTNOTES

1. *Matthew 15:2; Mark 7:3-5.*

2. *The writings* (**Kethubim**) *are the books of Psalms, Proverbs, Job, Song of Songs, Ruth, Lamentations, Ecclesiastes, Esther, Daniel, Ezra, Nehemiah, and 1 & 2 Chronicles.*

3. *The former prophets* (**Nebi'im Rishomim**) *are Joshua, Judges, 1 and 2 Samuel, and 1 and 2 Kings; the later prophets* (**Nebi'im Achronim**) *are Isaiah, Jeremiah, Ezekiel, and The Twelve Minor Prophets.*

4. *Russell, p. 161.*

5. *Josephus,* **Antiquities of the Jews,** *13.10.6.*

6. *Russell, p. 118.*

7. *M. Aboth 1:1.*

8. *Samuel Umen,* **Pharisaism and Jesus** *(New York: The Philosophical Library, Inc., 1963), p. 13.*

9. *Sandmel, p. 115.*

10. *Russell, p. 161.*

11. *Ibid.*

12. *Umen, p. 15.*

13. *Ibid., p. 17.*

14. *Ibid.*

15. *Ibid., p. 9.*

16. *Ibid., p. 15.*

17. *M. Aboth 3:14.*

18. *Russell, p. 161.*

19. *Mark 7:3.*

20. *Leviticus 11.*

21. *Deuteronomy 14:22.*

22. *Matthew 23:23.*

23. *Umen, p. 15.*

24. *Deuteronomy 24:1-4.*

25. *Umen, p. 15.*

26. *Ibid., pp. 15-16.*

27. *Matthew 15:3-6.*

CHAPTER THREE
QUESTIONS

1. What did the charge that Jesus transgressed the tradition of the fathers mean?

2. List some situations in which a person can declare Scripture to be his authority, but fail to live by its authority.

3. Who were the *diaspora?* What distinctive religious problem did they face as Jews?

4. Explain the two ways that the Pharisees used to determine proper religious authority when the Torah was silent.

5. Discuss the Pharisees' concept of tradition.

6. What were the objectives of the oral law? Discuss the relationship between tradition and the Torah.

7. Show how tradition sought to preserve the Torah in the following instances:
   A. The use of decrees
   B. The use of enactments

8. Explain the flaw in the Pharisees' use of the oral law in their attempt to preserve the written law.

THOUGHT QUESTION

List some traditional practices in the Lord's church today. How is a good traditional practice distinguished from a poor traditional practice?

CHAPTER FOUR
THE "OLD" ORAL LAW

It is fortunate that a person interested in Jewish traditional laws easily can make a study of oral law positions by reading the *Mishnah* (Herbert Danby, trans.: Oxford University Press, 1964). The *Mishnah* has been used by orthodox Jews for centuries. While there is some question about the date it was compiled, it is regarded as reflecting the Jewish oral law from the first and second centuries. It is indexed, readily allowing one to study oral law positions on a particular subject of interest. It is a single volume, and it can be obtained through a religious bookstore. Though one will have to learn some unfamiliar terms and words, he quickly can see the process used to interpret Scripture and to determine the intent of Scripture. Not only is such study interesting, but it also is enlightening in helping a person understand Jewish thoughts and actions reflected in the gospels.

The Sabbath

To illustrate the nature and function of the oral law as used by the Pharisees, consider the Torah commandment concerning the Sabbath day, Saturday.

> *Remember the sabbath day, to keep it holy. Six days shalt thou labor, and do thy work; but the seventh day is a sabbath unto Jehovah thy God: in it thou shalt not do any work, thou, nor thy son, nor thy daughter, nor thy man-servant, nor thy maid-servant, nor thy cattle, nor thy stranger within thy gates: for in six days Jehovah made heaven and earth, the sea, and all that in them is, and rested the seventh day: wherefore Jehovah blessed the seventh day and hallowed it.*[1]

In this commandment two things are obvious: the Sabbath must be kept holy; it is kept holy by refraining from work. Both of these facts are simple, easily understood. However, there is also an obvious difficulty in keeping this commandment. Before one can hallow the Sabbath by refraining from work, he must know what constitutes work. What is work? What activities constitute work? Specifically, what could one do and not do on the Sabbath?

These are essential, valid questions. To obey the law they must be answered. Yet, the written law itself did not define work. As important and essential as keeping the Sabbath was to the Jews, amazingly the Torah gave little information about how to define work. As this law is reaffirmed in other places in the Torah, it gives few insights into what work was. The seriousness of the law is declared in the fact that the person who violated the Sabbath by working "shall surely be put to death."[2] The Sabbath was to be observed in plowing time and in harvest time.[3] This implied one was not to plow or harvest on the Sabbath. Kindling a fire on the Sabbath also was prohibited.[4] Gathering sticks on the Sabbath was a work violation of the Sabbath.[5]

The absence of a comprehensive definition of work within the Torah created a significant problem for a conscientious Jew. If picking up sticks or lighting a fire constituted work and a violation of the Sabbath, what else violated the Sabbath? Could one tie his sandals? water the livestock? walk to a friend's home? If there was a true emergency situation, did this same law apply to the emergency situation? How could a person determine what work was? Under what circumstances, if any, could an exception be made?

"Going Out"

Since traditional or oral law determined the intent of the Torah and applied that intent to current life, it accepted the task of defining work. The detailed degree to which it defined work in all situations is an excellent example of the nature and purpose of the oral law. The sections "Shabbath" and "Erubin" in the *Mishnah* are devoted to regulations concerning the Sabbath.

In regard to hallowing the Sabbath, the Torah declared, "Let no man go out of his place" on the Sabbath.[6] The oral law first defined what constituted "going out." If a tailor accidentally carried a needle with him, on his person, on the Sabbath, or if a scribe carried a pen with him, each violated the Sabbath because each was carrying the tools of his trade.[7] One could not search his clothes for fleas nor read by lamplight.[8] A schoolteacher could not even read, for that was his work, but his pupils could read.[9] One could not sell merchandise to a

36

Gentile nor help him load supplies on his donkey unless the Gentile had time to reach his destination before the Sabbath began.[10]

There were differing rabbinic judgments regarding some of the regulations. Renowned rabbis had their own followings or schools. The followers or disciples of the rabbi lived by his judgments. Often noted rabbis disagreed with each other over certain details of the oral law. When there was a conflicting view, the *Mishnah* gave each view and associated each with the school of the particular rabbi. For example, the School of Shammai declared one could not soak something in dye on Friday unless the article had time to be completely soaked prior to the beginning of the Sabbath at sunset Friday; the School of Hillel said such was permissible even if the soaking was not complete by sunset.[11] Remember, the Sabbath began at sunset Friday and ended at sunset Saturday. In defining "going out" there were numerous injunctions concerning tasks begun on Friday which could not be completed prior to sunset.

Common Tasks

The regulations concerning common, daily tasks and chores which could not be permitted on the Sabbath seem endless. There are numerous regulations about lighting the Sabbath lamp.[12] Those regulations include what kind of oil could be used in the lamp and with what the lamp could be lighted. A second container could not be joined to the lamp prior to the Sabbath to prolong the oil supply and lamplight on the Sabbath[13] If a man put the lamp out to protect himself from thieves or evil spirits, or to allow a sick person to sleep, he had not violated the Sabbath. If he put the lamp out to save oil or the wick, he had violated the Sabbath.[14]

An egg could not be placed beside a hot kettle to cook, nor could it be buried in hot sand or the dust of the road to roast.[15] Cold water could not be placed in a hot kettle to warm, but cold water could be added to hot water to make it lukewarm.[16] Spices could not be added to a container of boiling food, but they could be added to hot food on a plate.[17]

There were numerous regulations on how hot food could be covered,[18] what could be carried by an animal,[19] what a woman could carry including articles of dress,[20] and what a man could carry.[21] One sandal alone could not be worn unless a person had a wounded foot.[22] A person could wear a garter, but not an ankle chain.[23] A one-legged man could use his wooden stump, but not a stool or pads.[24]

There are thirty-nine classes of work which are listed in Shabbath 7:2. If a man found he had unknowingly violated a Sabbath regulation numerous times, he offered only one sin offering. If he consciously violated a regulation on many Sabbaths, he was liable for every Sabbath violated. If all the violations were within one category of work, he was liable for only one sin offering.[25]

Emergencies

There are various regulations about emergencies. Shabbath 16 gives the following instructions concerning a fire. Scripture could be saved from burning by carrying it a prescribed distance from the fire. If a fire broke out in a home, enough food could be saved for three meals if the fire occurred on Friday night, or for two meals if the fire occurred on Saturday morning, or for only one meal if it occurred on Saturday afternoon. However, food which was stored in a basket could be carried out in the basket regardless of the amount in the container. Clothes could be taken out of the house to save them if the person wore them out. He could call to friends to come help him get them out in this manner. He could run back in to save some more clothes as often as he wished. If a chest, a box, or a cupboard caught on fire, it could be smothered with a hide because the hide would not burn, and one would not be lighting a fire on the Sabbath. If a fire was burning in a room, a person could gather clay vessels and stack them to create a barrier to keep the fire from speading to the rest of the room, but he could not put the fire out. A Gentile could come put the fire out as long as the Jew did not ask him or tell him not to.

Shabbath 23:4-5 gives the following instructions in the event of a death. The body could be washed and anointed, but not moved. If the body was on a mattress, the mattress could be pulled from beneath it to allow it to lie on the cool sand and to be preserved longer. The chin could be tied closed before it fell open, but not afterward. They could not close the eyes of the dead one at any time on the Sabbath. In fact, one who closed the eyes of a dying person prior to the person's death on any day was a "shedder of blood" because in doing so he was preventing the soul from departing. At nightfall on Saturday, funeral wrappings for the body and a coffin could be obtained. If perchance the family found a coffin which had been built by a Gentile on the Sabbath for a Gentile, and a grave dug on the Sabbath for a Gentile, that coffin and grave could be used to bury the deceased Jew. However, if the coffin had been built and the grave dug on the Sabbath by a Gentile for a Jew, it could not be used.

The section Erubin deals with determining Sabbath limits. Many of these regulations are quite detailed. For example, if a man had been on a journey and darkness caught him on Friday evening prior to reaching his home, and if he saw a familar tree, he could say, "Let my Sabbath resting place be at its root." With that statement he could proceed to the root of the tree, though the Sabbath had begun, traveling up to 1,333 feet. Once he reached the root, he was allowed to travel an additional 1,333 feet to reach his house.[26] If a man was sent to travel beyond the Sabbath limit on a permissible errand such as bearing witness to the new moon or saving a life, and if at arrival he was informed that the needful act had already been done, he was permitted to move 1,333 feet in any direction to find and enter his place of Sabbath rest.[27] If a man fell asleep on a journey and awoke after sunset Friday evening, he was permitted to move 1,333 feet in any direction.[28]

These examples are sufficient to illustrate the nature and intent of oral law. The Torah prohibited work on the Sabbath. To obey that law, work had to be defined. The oral law defined work with the intent of guaranteeing proper obedience to the Sabbath law and of prohibiting violation of the Sabbath law.

The Effect of the Oral Law

The endless, detailed regulations defined work, but they also created some problems. (1) They turned obedience to God into legalism. Obedience amounted to no more than keeping regulations. (2) The legalism created formalism. It was not enough to be versed in the teaching of Scripture. One must also be versed in the teachings of the oral law. Following the form of the oral law became a substitute for following the teachings of Scripture itself. One could keep the form created by the regulations and live in ignorance of the heart and concern of the Scripture. (3) Many of the regulations had virtually nothing to do with Scripture itself. Some were nothing more than human judgments based on fragments of Scripture. (4) Some of the regulations were based on double standards which in themselves violated the intent of Scripture. Work done in behalf of a Jew by a Gentile was just as certainly work. Thus, with shrewdness and care, one could use the oral law to bypass the intent of the Torah.

The overall effect was to create a system of ritualism. It is certain that few of the common people understood the basis, the wherefores, and the whys of the myriad regulations imposed upon them. Only the rabbis and their schooled disciples understood the theological reasons for the existence of particular regulations. Thus, for the common man, it merely became the proposition of "learn the rules and keep them." Such created ritualism rather than meaningful, personal response to God.

One easily can see why the Pharisees constantly condemned Jesus about such matters as acts of healing on the Sabbath. It is also obvious why Jesus' challenges made them so angry.

CHAPTER FOUR
FOOTNOTES

1. *Exodus 20:8-11.*
2. *Exodus 31:1-17.*
3. *Exodus 34:21.*
4. *Exodus 35:2-3.*
5. *Numbers 15:32-36.*
6. *Exodus 16:29.*
7. *M. Shabbath 1:3.*
8. *M. Shabbath 1:3.*
9. *M. Shabbath 1:3.*
10. *M. Shabbath 1:7.*
11. *M. Shabbath 1:5.*
12. *M. Shabbath 2:1-3.*
13. *M. Shabbath 2:4.*
14. *M. Shabbath 2:5.*
15. *M. Shabbath 3:3.*
16. *M. Shabbath 3:5.*
17. *M. Shabbath 3:5.*
18. *M. Shabbath 4.*
19. *M. Shabbath 5.*
20. *M. Shabbath 6.*
21. *M. Shabbath 6.*
22. *M. Shabbath 6:2.*
23. *M. Shabbath 6:4.*
24. *M. Shabbath 6:8.*
25. *M. Shabbath 7:1.*

26. *M. Erubin 4:7.*

27. *M. Erubin 4:3.*

28. *M. Erubin 4:5.*

CHAPTER FOUR
QUESTIONS

1. What is the *Mishnah*?

2. Read Exodus 20:8-11 and discuss the Sabbath commandment.

3. What day was (is) the Sabbath? How was it kept holy?

4. What basic difficulty existed in obeying that law?

5. Read the following passages and discuss the information each gives concerning the Sabbath:
   A. Exodus 31:12-17
   B. Exodus 34:21
   C. Exodus 35:2-3
   D. Numbers 15:32-36

6. Illustrate how the oral law defined "going out" on the Sabbath. (If a *Mishnah* is available, report on some of the unusual Sabbath laws.)

7. Discuss some of the common tasks the oral law forbade on the Sabbath.

8. What could a person do on the Sabbath in the following circumstances?
   A. His home caught on fire.
   B. A person in the house died.
   C. He was on a trip and failed to make his destination by sunset Friday.

9. Discuss the four problems created by the oral law.

10. Explain the overall effect of the oral law.

THOUGHT QUESTION

How can the Christian life be reduced to a series of meaningless rules and regulations to be kept?

CHAPTER FIVE

THE "NEW" ORAL LAW

Because the Pharisees and Jesus were continuously in conflict during Jesus' ministry, the Pharisees symbolize religious villians to most Christians. Most Christians would affirm that New Testament Christians of today and the Pharisees of Jesus' day have little in common. The truth is that the restoration church of today and the Pharisees of the first century hold much in common. The Pharisees held Scripture in reverence. They believed in the adequacy of Scripture and its sufficiency to regulate all life. They unquestionably accepted Scripture as being from God. Their religious lives were founded on the belief that Scripture could be interpreted and applied to the real questions of current times and religious issues. Christians from the restoration movement hold identical positions. They revere Scripture, believing in its adequacy and sufficiency to regulate all life. They unquestionably accept it as being from God. They found their lives on the conviction that Scripture can be interpreted properly and applied to the real questions of current times and religious issues.

Shared Attitudes and Outlooks

New Testament Christians share far more with the Pharisees than a common view of Scripture. As the Pharisee, the Christian often blurs the distinction between common interpretations of the meaning of Scripture and Scripture itself. Often an accepted interpretation of a meaning or an intent of Scripture is regarded as being actual Scripture. Rarely do many Christians view interpretations as being interpretations. As the Pharisees, many Christians will defend an accepted interpretation as emphatically and emotionally as they will defend Scripture itself.

43

In the minds of most Christians, the word "interpretation" is not an acceptable or appropriate word to be used in reference to Scripture. The old addage, "It means what it says and says what it means," created the continuing conviction that Scripture never needs to be interpreted. That conviction is at best an oversimplification. Every preacher and Bible class teacher spends most of his teaching time explaining the meaning of the passage under consideration and applying that meaning to present needs and questions. The basic purpose of every commentary is to explain the meaning of the book under consideration. Interpretation is the process of determining the meaning of the text. There are many types of both good and bad interpretation. Conjecture, uninformed opinion, educated opinion, convictions based on study and research, and conclusions drawn from exegesis are all forms of interpretation. Interpretation always asks two basic questions: what does this Scripture mean? how does the meaning apply to life today? Every student of Scripture interprets Scripture. Meaningful study is impossible without it. The true goal of interpretation is to determine accurately the meaning the Scripture had when it was written by the original, inspired writer. That is the meaning one wishes to apply to current questions and religious needs.

Interpreting the Scriptures for the purpose of making accurate application of Scripture to existing problems and questions has been a part of the restoration movement from its earliest days. After years of involvement with and leadership in the restoration movement, Alexander Campbell wrote *The Christian System*. This work was devoted to setting forth proper restoration concepts concerning a broad range of Bible subjects. In the preface Campbell wrote,

> *Having also considered the most vulnerable side of every great question, and re-examined the terms and phrase which have occasioned the most opposition and controversy, whether from our own pen or that of any of our brethren, our aim is now to offer the public a more matured view of such capital principles as are necessary to the right interpretation of the Holy Scripture . . .* [1]

Concern for proper interpretation of Scripture will forever be a part of the restoration church. Among more recent writings regarding Biblical interpretation are J. D. Thomas' *We Be Brethren* and Thomas B. Warren's *When Is An "Example" Binding?* In his preface, Thomas stated that all in the brotherhood have legalistic tendencies.[2] "This author (Thomas) feels that some who accept the same conclusions he does have in the past used very unsound methods of interpretation and perhaps have been guided by a great deal of prejudice."[3] Among his reasons for writing his book, Warren noted, "One must learn not only what the Bible *says*, but also what it *means*. . ."[4]

The Pharisees were concerned with two basic problems: (1) determining proper authority, and (2) applying the intent of Scripture to current life. New Testament Christians have the same two concerns. The Pharisees' concerns were created by the changing world. There was a need to deal with existing religious problems which written Scripture specifically did not address. Their current religious questions and needs had to be harmonized with the teachings of Scripture. Today's Christian faces precisely the same situation. The Pharisees did not intend for their interpretations to violate or set aside written Scripture. Neither does today's Christian. These combined concerns and needs produced an authoritative oral law for the Pharisees. The same combined concerns and needs also have produced an oral law for the restoration church. The old oral law was "the tradition of the elders"; the new oral law is the "tradition of the preachers." Unfortunately, the Pharisees often regarded faithfulness to the interpretations as being more important than faithfulness to the Scriptures. Sadly, the same problem often exists in the restoration church.

The Church and the Problem

As the restoration movement began, the motivating issue and unifying concern was acknowledging the sufficiency and unifying power of the sole authority of Scripture. It was a good, sound, admirable concern filled with the promise of spiritual blessing including unity. While the movement was quite young, a serious question arose which became a perpetual, troubling question. That question is quite alive and vigorous today. The question was, "How is the true meaning of Scripture determined?" The answer to that question was critical because it determined the answers to related, equally important questions: who has the right to determine the meaning of the Scripture? Who has the right to declare the intent of Scripture? Who has the right to bind the meaning and intent of Scripture? Who are "the faithful"? At the heart of all these questions are proper authority and the criteria for determining faithfulness.

Just as with the Sadducees and Pharisees, factions within the restoration church began opposing each other over the answers to those questions, and the struggle has never ceased. The struggle became divisive over the question of the use of instrumental music in worship. Two basic views of authority formed the dividing line in determining the meaning and intent of Scripture. View one: anything not authorized by New Testament Scripture is unacceptable. View two: anything not specifically condemned by New Testament Scripture is acceptable. These were two approaches to determining the meaning of Scripture, of interpreting the intent of Scripture, and of determining who were "the faithful."

This merely began the process of factions opposing factions within the restoration church. Within those congregations who accepted the view that New Testament authorization must exist, there have been endless factions. Each new faction rejects and ostracizes all other factions. It is sure it has found, understood, and accepted the true meaning of Scripture concerning a question which is *the* issue. Its interpretation of the *key* passages is regarded as Scripture itself. The faction is "the faithful," and all others are transgressors. A whole new set of rules and regulations come into existence to safeguard "the truth" which their interpretation declares. This produces another segment of authoritative oral law. With each new faction, the group is certain it holds the true meaning of Scripture and accurately complies with Biblical authority. What each faction is unconsciously declaring is that each is convinced its interpretations are valid, and everyone else's are not.

Some of the factions existing in the restoration church are widely known. Each claims to be "the faithful" and ostracizes all others who became Christians in the very same manner by respecting and obeying the very same New Testament instructions. Most of these factions are known by that which they oppose and reject: congregational cooperation, Bible classes within the congregation, the use of printed literature in the assemblies, and the use of more than one communion cup. The basic issue is always the same: how do you determine the meaning of Scripture? How do you apply the intent of Scripture? How do you apply the intent of Scripture to today's needs and situations? Who has the right to declare and to bind that meaning and intent on others?

This situation has created a powerful system for determining truth and demanding compliance which has little to do with written Scripture. First, Christians commonly base their convictions on the views of influential preachers just as the Pharisees appealed to influential rabbis. One is more likely to hear Christians discussing positions of influential, outspoken preachers regarding difficult religious questions than to hear them discussing Scripture. The Christian is more likely to define his "position" on the basis of the "position" of a respected preacher than on studied Scripture.

Second, the most common concerns one hears Christians discussing are the "issues." Faithfulness, Christian existence, the work of Christians as individuals and the church, and what the church needs to preach and to "stand for" are determined by the current "issues." The Pharisees also pushed what they regarded to be issues. Often, issues are examined more comprehensively than Scripture. In fact, the only Scripture examined is that which is deemed to be relevant to the issue.

Third, like the Pharisees, many Christians have devised a labeling system. In the first century and today the labels varied from group to group. Three prominent, widely-used labels are conservative, liberal, and anti. As with first-century Judaism, there is no standard definition for the labels. In the first century (using today's terminology) the Pharisee regarded the Essenes as anti, and the Essenes regarded the Pharisees as liberal. Today one person's conservative is another person's anti. Depending on the different perspectives of others, a person can be a conservative to one group and a liberal to another. If "you" disagree with "me" concerning the meaning and application of a passage "I" regard basic and critical, "you" are either liberal or anti. Everyone prefers to be labeled conservative, for conservative (whatever its definition) equals faithful. To be labeled liberal is anathama. Faith, knowledge of the Scripture, and devotion to the Word ususally do not determine the label a person wears. Commonly, one is labeled on the basis of the judgments and accusations of others.

Fourth, as with the Pharisees, "watchdogs of faithfulness" have been appointed and exercise considerable influence. Usually these persons are self-appointed. Their ability to create questions in the minds and thinking of others even in regard to honorable, scriptural matters forces other Christians, preachers, congregations, and even schools to be extremely self-conscious. If an influential watchdog sounds an alarm by merely being suspicious that there may be a liberal trend in certain quarters, irreparable harm can result even if the suspicions prove groundless. The watchdog may apologize, but the question mark created in the minds of others remains. Many of the alarms sounded by the watchdogs have to do with violations of accepted oral laws.

The real tragedy is this: almost none of the factions exist because of disagreement over the actual commands or specific statements of written Scripture. The majority of problems occur because of the extensive system of unwritten oral laws devised to declare the meaning and intent of Scripture.

The New Oral Law

The oral law so influential in the restoration church today does not exist in decrees but in "positions" on the "issues." A position is declared to be the correct stand on the *intent* of Scripture. The passages to which appeal is made concerning the issue often do not actually, plainly, directly say what the position declares. The collective meaning of the passages shows that the position is consistent with the intent of the passages. A position declares, "If the New Testament writer had been writing today, this is what he would have said about this matter."

The reason necessitating the creation of positions is the existence of moral and religious questions today which did not exist in the New Testament times. There are many oral law positions which have been accepted by so many for so long that they are regarded as being Scripture itself.

Current religious and moral questions that frequently demand an answer include these: appropriate dress for women, the use of the church building, the use of translations, the worship format or order, "disfellowshipping" congregations, and Christian participation in warfare. There were no bikinis in the first century. The brevity of a woman's clothing is never discussed in the New Testament. In 1 Peter 3:3 "immodest apparel" deals with the practice of a woman wearing too much clothes. It was the practice of a prideful woman flaunting her affluence. There were no church buildings owned by congregations until well after the first century. Not one passage in context deals with the use of a church building. In the New Testament the "church" never referred to a building. Although translations existed and were used by Jesus and New Testament writers,[5] not one word is said about "approved" translations or the practice of translating Scripture. Not one format for worship from a single congregation is preserved in Scripture. The word "disfellowship" is not found in the text. Never is one congregation disciplined by other congregations. In Revelation 2 and 3, the faithful Smyrna and Philadelphia congregations are not instructed to discipline the loveless Ephesus congregation, the immoral Thyatira congregation, or the dead Sardis congregation. That was the Lord's work. Only individuals of the congregations were disciplined by the congregation. In the first-century Roman empire the possibility of Christians of one nation being in combat against Christians of another nation did not exist. That moral dilemma was never discussed. Romans 13 deals with civil obedience and payment of taxes, not military involvement.

Yet, many congregations and Christian individuals take strong, inflexible positions on each of these matters. Many judge the faithfulness of others on the basis of others' agreement or disagreement with their positions. They do so because they, through interpretation, have determined the "correct" intent of Scripture in these matters. They regard their interpretations as being as authoritative as Scripture itself. This is their oral law. Their objective in all this is: (1) to enforce the intent of the Scripture; (2) to make Scripture applicable to today's needs and questions. In these two matters, the restoration church is like the Pharisees.

CHAPTER FIVE
FOOTNOTES

1. *Alexander Campbell,* **The Christian System** *(Standard Publishing Company, Cincinnati, 1901), p. xv.*

2. *J. D. Thomas,* **We Be Brethren** *(Biblical Research Press: Abilene, Texas, 1958), p. viii.*

3. *Ibid.*

4. *Thomas B. Warren,* **When Is An "Example" Binding?** *(National Christian Press: Jonesboro, AR., 1975), p. 7.*

5. *In the first century A.D. (and before) an interpreter orally paraphrased the reading of the Hebrew text in the synagogue. This paraphrase was called a* **targum.** *In time Targums were written. New Testament writings quote passages from some Targum sources. The Septuagint is the Greek translation of the Old Testament. Many New Testament quotations from the Old Testament are from this translation. The books of Luke and Hebrews make extensive use of it. F.F. Bruce,* **The Books and The Parchments,** *revised edition (Fleming H. Revell Company: Westwood, N.J., 1963), pp. 133-162.*

CHAPTER FIVE
QUESTIONS

1. List some of the views the Pharisees and the restoration church have in common.

2. What problem regarding Scripture do some Christians hold in common with the Pharisees?

3. Concerning interpreting the Scripture:
   A. Give some common forms of interpretation.

B. Give some examples of good and bad interpretation.
C. What two questions does interpretation ask?
D. What is the proper goal of interpretation?
4. What two basic religious concerns did the Pharisees have? Do Christians have the same concerns?
5. What is the oral law of the restoration church today?
6. Regarding the early restoration movement:
   A. What was the motivating issue and unifying concern?
   B. What serious question arose?
   C. What other related, important questions also arose?
   D. What question divided the restoration movement?
   E. What two views of authority were held when the division arose?
7. Why do divisive factions exist in the restoration church today?
8. What system for determining truth and demanding compliance (aside from Scripture) exists in the church?
9. What is a "position"?
   A. Why are "positions" needed?
   B. How can "positions" be used harmfully? Give examples.

THOUGHT QUESTION

Why do factions find it necessary to establish their own oral laws?

CHAPTER SIX

PHARISAISM
IN THE EARLY CHURCH

The influence of first-century Pharisaism was not restricted to Judaism and Jewish people. Scripture indicates that converted Pharisees were a strong, distinct voice in the early church. The Pharisaic philosophy did not die in converted Pharisees when they accepted Christ. In their own thinking they found it quite compatible to hold to Pharisaism and to faith in Christ. They were committed to being devout Christians and devout Pharisees. More importantly, they were determined to mold Christianity according to the principles and dictates of Pharisaism. As a result, they created a problem which threatened the worldwide existence of the church and Christ's mission as the universal Savior of man.

Pharisaic Influence in the Church

Acts 15 documents the existence of this group in the Jerusalem church. It also declares their basic conviction and reveals the power of their influence.

When Paul returned from his first missionary journey, he gave a complete report about his work to the church of Antioch.[1] As he "tarried no little time"[2] with the church, he confronted a serious problem. Because of the seriousness of the problem, Barnabas and Paul had "no small dissention and questioning"[3] with those from Judea who created the crisis. The crux of the crisis was quite simple: some Judean Christians declared that Gentile Christians who refused to accept Jewish circumcision could not be saved.[4] They declared that Gentiles who were baptized believers were yet unsaved until they accepted the Jewish rite of circumcision. The Jewish Christians who taught this view seemingly declared the teaching had the sanction and approval of the apostles.[5] Their position caused Gentile converts to question their salvation.

Had this position been adopted, the church would have become solely a Jewish institution. Christianity would have been little more than a reformation movement in Judaism. Limited indoctrination in Judaism and the acceptance of the rites of proselytism would have been a prerequisite for the conversion of any non-Jew. This would have created a significant obstacle to the spread of Christianity among the Gentiles. This teaching also had immediate consequences. It meant many Gentiles Christians at Antioch were not saved, and it meant few of the Gentile converts of Asia Minor were saved.

When the matter could not be resolved in the discussions at Antioch, it was referred to the apostles and elders in Jerusalem. Paul fully understood the seriousness of the issue. He realized an apostolic pronouncement from him would carry little force because the Judaizing teachers doubted the validity of his apostolic status.[6] The only appropriate means for resolving the issue without major harm was a consensus declaration by all apostles. When Paul, Barnabas, and other representatives of the Antioch congregation arrived in Jerusalem, Paul and Barnabas made a complete report on "all things God had done with them."[7]

Acts 15:5 states there were converted Pharisees at the meeting who endorsed and supported the position of the Judaizing teachers. They insisted it was needful to circumcise Gentile converts *and* to charge these Gentile converts to keep the law of Moses. It is possible that the Judaizing teachers at Antioch came from this faction of the Jerusalem Christians. Note the influence of these converted Pharisees in the Jerusalem church. (1) They were a recognized, distinct group within the congregation. They were a distinct voice representing a definite position. They were a definite voice within the church. (2) Their influence was such that their position and argument could not be ignored. Their position had to be evaluated on the basis of specific evidence. Their position was rejected, but only after it was shown to be in obvious conflict with the intent of Christ and the Spirit. (3) The rejection of their position in this matter did not end their influence in the Jerusalem church. Much later after Paul completed two additional mission journeys, there were "many thousands" in the Jerusalem congregation who were "zealous for the law."[8] Because of their influence the elders urged Paul to allay their suspicions about him by taking a Jewish vow.[9]

The Pharisaic Christians' Concern

The Pharisees of the first century were evangelistic.[10] Their view

52

was that God was one as people are one. When all nations understood the oneness of God, all nations would become the mountain of the Lord and learn His ways. Thus the nations needed to be taught the Torah.[11] This view motivated them to seek proselytes.

The evangelistic efforts of Judaism, especially of the *diaspora*, resulted in two types of responses from the Gentiles. There were numerous Gentiles who believed in the one living God, who accepted certain elements of the ceremonial law, and who attended worship, but who did not become proselytes.[12] These Gentiles were known as the "God-fearers," the "devout Greeks," or the "worshipping Greeks."[13] When Paul spoke in the synagogue at Antioch of Pisidia, he began his address with these words: "Men of Israel, and ye that fear God . . ."[14] Both Jewish and Gentile listeners were specifically mentioned again: "Brethren, children of the stock of Abraham, and those among you that fear God . . ."[15] Cornelius was such a person.[16]

Other receptive Gentiles became proselytes. The proselyte was a Gentile who had responded to Judaism by complete conversion. The rites of proselytism involved three parts: circumcision (for male converts), a ceremonial washing similar to baptism, and the offering of a sacrifice at the temple.[17] A non-Jew converted to Judaism in this manner was regarded "in every respect as a Jew."[18]

Jesus acknowledged the Pharisees' evangelistic zeal for proselyting Gentiles.[19] He said they would compass land and sea to make one proselyte. The audience who heard the first gospel sermon included Jews and proselytes.[20] One of the Christian men chosen to minister to the Jerusalem widows was Nicolaus, a proselyte of Antioch.[21] After Paul spoke to the synagogue at Antioch of Pisidia, many of the Jews and many of the devout proselytes followed him and Barnabas.[22]

The most receptive people to Paul's evangelistic efforts were the God-fearers. Invariably Paul began teaching in a community by speaking in the local synagogue. Commonly, the God-fearing Gentiles received his message with great joy. These devout Greeks were receptive to the message of salvation in Christ. They were present at the synagogue of Iconium[23], the synagogue in Corinth[24], and the synagogue of Athens.[25] Among them were numbered such persons as Lydia[26] and Titus Justus.[27] Large numbers of them responded at Thessalonica[28], at Iconium[29], and at Beroea.[30].

The evangelistic Jews were outraged at the response of the God-fearers to the gospel because this gave the Gentiles a shortcut to the full blessings of complete relationship with God. Gentiles who were baptized into Christ were thereby passing the Jewish rites for a proselyte. They were acting as and being regarded as full children of

God. The Pharisees adamantly maintained that it was impossible for Gentiles to be children of God unless they first became a proselyte.

This was the heart of the issue in the Jerusalem church in Acts 15. Converts from the Pharisees strongly maintained that Gentiles had to become a proselyte before they were suitable candidates for salvation in Christ.

The view of the Pharisees, in and out of the church, was that salvation by grace made it too simple for Gentiles to become people of God. Grace made salvation too easy. The idea that a believing Jew and a believing Gentile by grace could be equally righteous before God was unacceptable. Through the law the Jews had "paid their dues"; the Gentiles had not.

The Attitude Lives

Christians who are skeptical about the conversion of others still exist in the church. News of rapid conversions on a foreign mission field causes them to think aloud,"What's wrong? People do not respond that quickly. Something is not right — something must be too easy." If someone responds knowledgeably but quickly to the gospel in the congregation, again they say, "He does not know what he is doing. He knows too little about church teachings and doctrines. Because he found it so easy to respond, he will not last."

These are the Christians who strongly feel there should be an approved indoctrination program before baptism Understanding one's sinfulness, the atoning death of Jesus, the power of the resurrection, and the forgiveness of sin through His blood is not sufficient for baptism. People need to be taught all the "correct" doctrines and positions in the church first. Only if they understand and accept the "correct" positions first are they ready for baptism. The way to "protect" the church is to be certain conversion is not too easy. Jesus' instruction in Matthew 28:19-20 was first to baptize believers and then to teach them to observe all things He had commanded. Fortunately, the Ethiopian eunuch and the Philippian jailer did not encounter a Phariasaic Christian.

CHAPTER SIX
FOOTNOTES

1. *Acts 14:27.*
2. *Acts 14:28.*

3. *Acts 15:2.*
4. *Acts 15:1.*
5. *Acts 15:24.*
6. *Galatians 1,2.*
7. *Acts 15:4.*
8. *Acts 21:20.*
9. *Acts 21:23-24.*
10. *Matthew 23:15.*
11. *Isaiah 2:2; 56:6-7.*
12. *Kittel and Friedrich, "prosalutos," 6:731.*
13. *Ibid.*
14. *Acts 13:6.*
15. *Acts 13:26.*
16. *Acts 10:2.*
17. *Kittel and Friedrich, "prosalutos," 6:738.*
18. *Ibid., p. 739.*
19. *Matthew 23:15.*
20. *Acts 2:10.*
21. *Acts 6:5.*
22. *Acts 13:43.*
23. *Acts 14:1.*
24. *Acts 18:4.*
25. *Acts 17:17.*
26. *Acts 16:14.*
27. *Acts 18:7.*
28. *Acts 17:4.*
29. *Acts 14:1.*
30. *Acts 17:12.*

CHAPTER SIX
QUESTIONS

1. Use Acts 15 to discuss the Pharisees' influence in the early church.
   A. What was the problem?
   B. What did this view mean in regard to most Gentile converts?
   C. If this view had been adopted, what would have been the consequence?

2. How significant were the Phariasaic Christians within the Jerusalem church?

3. Why were the Pharisees evangelistic?

4. Who were the "God-fearers"?

5. Who were proselytes? List some instances in which proselytes are mentioned in the New Testament.

6. Why were the Jews outraged by the response of the "God-fearers" to the gospel?

7. Explain how the same attitudes live in some Christians today.

THOUGHT QUESTION

Why are some Christians fearful and resentful of scriptural lessons on salvation by faith and grace?

CHAPTER SEVEN

THE CONFLICT BETWEEN PHARISAISM AND THE GOSPEL

It is obvious in the book of Acts that Paul spent a lot of time teaching in synagogues.[1] Acts also makes it evident that the gospel quickly found itself in conflict with Pharisaic views;[2] Pharisaism was hostile to the point of violence against those who presented the gospel.[3]

Why? What was the basic issue which placed Pharisaism and the gospel in a position of violent confrontation? Within the restoration church, the most probable answer given would be, "The basic issue was the legalism which characterized Pharisaism." This view declares that the Pharisees' devotion to the letter of the law and to the concept of salvation by works placed Pharisaism in legalistic opposition to the grace proclaimed by the gospel.

The Issue

The conflict between Pharisaism and the gospel was focused in two questions. Question one: how was God's grace dispensed? Was God's grace dispensed through the Mosaical law or through Jesus? Pharisaism rejected Jesus as the avenue of grace. Question two: what role did obedience play in a person's salavation? Aside from Jesus not being the avenue of divine grace, Pharisaism regarded Christian teachings as having the wrong concept of the role of obedience in making a person righteous.

In the Pharisaic view, a Jew who kept the law of Moses was righteous and justified because (1) he was a Jew, and (2) he did approved works. It was the act of keeping the law which made the Jew righteous. Righteousness was not the result of a divine act in human life made possible by proper faith, but the result of collective human

57

acts in honoring the law's teachings, rituals, and ceremonies. Mosaical sacrifices were quite sufficient for atonement.

Paul, the former Pharisee, taught a concept of righteousness by faith which stood in complete contrast to the Pharisaic concept of righteousness. Paul acknowledged that a primary reason for his leaving Judaism and entering Christ was this: he did not want a righteousness of his own which was produced by obedience to the law, but the righteousness which is from God and is produced by faith in Christ.[4] Paul was qualified to distinguish between those two concepts of righteousness because as a Pharisee he had been "blameless" in regard to "the righteousness which is in the law."[5] In discussing the fact that the crucified Jesus was a stumbling block to the Jews and foolishness to the Greeks, Paul declared that Christ Jesus "was made unto us. . . righteousness."[6] He is the means of our being seen by God as righteous. Jesus was "made to be sin on our behalf; that we might become the righteousness of God in him."[7] In this age of the new covenant through Christ, righteousness is revealed through faith, and the righteous live by faith.[8] This new righteousness made possible by and revealed through Christ (1) has been manifested apart from the law, (2) has the law and the prophets as its witnesses, and (3) exists through faith in Jesus Christ in all those who believe in Christ.[9] The Gentiles who did not have righteousness through the Mosaical law did attain righteousness by having faith in Christ.[10] Israel who had attempted to achieve righteousness through the law failed to arrive at a law of righteousness. They failed because they did not act by faith, but sought righteousness by works.[11]

The crux of the confrontation is quite evident: what role does obedience play in making one righteous? Pharisaism said obedience played the primary role. The Pharisees did not regard themselves as legalists in this issue. They believed in the essentiality of God's grace.[12] Aside from Jesus' identity as the Christ, the issue was this: does obedience appropriate the grace of God or does faith appropriate the grace of God?

A Continuing Issue

In this matter the parallel between the Pharisaic view and the view held by many New Testament Christians is chilling. Be it understood (1) that no faction of the restoration church today regards themselves as being legalists, and (2) that all factions would openly declare they believe in the essentiality of God's grace. However, many believe and strongly affirm that a New Testament Christian is righteous and justified before God because (1) he is a member of the restoration church, and (2) he is doing approved works. It is the act of obeying the right teachings which makes a member of Christ's church righteous. Righteousness is not the result of a divine act in human life made possible by proper faith, but the result of collective human acts in honoring the church's teachings and approved way of doing religious acts.

There continues to be a confrontation in the church between factions over the question of how a person can stand as righteous in God's eyes. The crux of the confrontation remains the same: what role does obedience play in making one righteous? The issue remains the same: does obedience appropriate the grace of God, or does faith appropriate the grace of God?

Those who conclude that obedience is the means of the Christian becoming righteous create the same problems which afflicted and blinded Pharisaism. Even though they affirm that the grace of God is essential, complete obedience is seen as essential to "meriting" that grace. Thus one becomes committed to trying to be "good enough" to "merit" grace through complete obedience to Christ. That view quickly degenerates into a legalism which is used to measure faithfulness, and into an attempt to earn the status of being righteous by doing a sufficient number of declared godly works. The position held due to this concept is the primary source of the searing, judgmental attitudes held by many in the restoration church. It is also the major reason so many members of the restoration church live with the continuous feeling of guilt and with the fear that they are not forgiven.

What Is The Role Of Obedience?

To properly understand the role of obedience, one must begin with a study of grace. Salvation by grace is a plain, undeniable truth clearly set forth in Scripture. The appearing of the grace of God brought salvation to all men.[13] Jew and Gentile alike shall be saved by the grace of Jesus.[14] Justification is freely obtained by God's grace through the redemption which exists in Christ Jesus.[15] The Christian has been saved by grace.[16]

Being saved by grace means salvation exists and has been obtained by the individual as the result of an unmerited act of God. God manifested His love by allowing Christ to die for Christians while they were still sinners.[17] In no sense does any saved person deserve that sacrifice. A person can do nothing before accepting Christ which makes him deserving of Christ's sacrifice. A person can do nothing after accepting Christ which makes him deserving of Christ's sacrifice.

59

Salvation by grace means there is no possible way for any person ever to be saved by earning salvation or by placing God in debt to himself. No act of obedience or collective acts of obedience can result in such earnings or divine indebtedness. That being true, salvation has to be and is specifically declared to be a gift.[18]

Do the facts that salvation cannot be earned and that salvation is a gift eliminate obedience? No! However, those facts do define the role of obedience. To understand the role of obedience, (1) one must understand the nature of grace, and (2) he must determine in what sense is salvation a gift.

Grace exists through Jesus Christ.[19] The Christian is able to "stand" by being in or under grace, and his access into grace is by faith.[20] No person can glory or boast in his salvation because it is by grace through faith; it is a gift to all Christians and a human achievement by no one.[21] The purpose the newly created Christian has in Christianity is to accomplish good works which were intended by God for the saved to perform.[22] God intended for the saved to do good works from the inception of His plan to save by grace through faith in Christ. Obviously, grace and obedience are not in opposition if each exists in its right role for its rightful purpose.

What kind of gift is salvation or eternal life? Three gospels, Acts, five epistles, and Revelation state it is an inheritance.[23] Jesus promised that those who made sacrifices for him would inherit eternal life.[24] Paul was sent as an apostle to the Gentiles to enable them to receive an inheritance for those sanctified by faith.[25] Christ makes Christians His heritage[26] and suited to be partakers of the inheritance.[27] That inheritance is incorruptible, undefiled, does not fade, and is reserved in heaven for the Christian.[28]

An inheritance is a gift which is not earned, but it is not a gift indiscriminately given to anyone. It is a gift given only to those who are qualified heirs as declared by the terms of the will. Only those qualified shall receive the gift. Christ has declared that anyone can become a qualified heir to be a recipient of the gift of salvation if the person will have faith in Christ and express that faith through repentance and baptism.[29] Faith, repentance, and baptism are never an attempt to earn salvation. They are expressions of compliance with the covenant or testament of Christ in becoming qualified heirs who have the full right to the gift.

Obedience serves three purposes. First, it expresses faith in the manner designated by Scripture to allow the sinner to become full heir in Christ. Second, it expresses the love of a Christian to Christ for the salvation he has been given and for the relationship with God in which he lives.[30] Third, it expresses his trust in God and Christ and Their promises.[31]

For the Christian, obedience is always an expression of love and faith. It is never an attempt to earn salvation or make oneself righteous through human achievement. In that understanding is the joy and the hope of the gospel of grace in Christ Jesus. Perfect obedience under Christ is just as impossible as perfect obedience under the Mosaical law. One reason which necessitated the coming of Jesus was the need to establish a way for people to become righteous which was not dependent on the human achievement of perfect obedience. That is and forever has been an impossibility! Righteousness by faith through grace makes it possible for every imperfect Christian who lives in faith to stand before God whole, justified, and forgiven.

CHAPTER SEVEN
FOOTNOTES

1. *Acts 13:15-16; 14:1; 17:1-2; 18:4; 19:8.*

2. *Acts 13:45; 14:2; 18:6; 19:9.*

3. *Acts 13:50; 14:4,5,19; 17:5-9; 18:12-13.*

4. *Philippians 3:9.*

5. *Philippians 3:5-6.*

6. *1 Corinthians 1:30.*

7. *2 Corinthians 5:21.*

8. *Romans 1:17.*

9. *Romans 3:21-22.*

10. *Romans 9:30.*

11. *Romans 9:31-32.*

12. *The concept of divine grace was known to first century A.D. Judaism and accepted by some Jewish sects. However, Judaism's concept differed significantly from the Christian concept. In the Dead Sea Scrolls hymn 13 L, 7:6-25, the author declared he owed everything to the grace of God; he could be saved by grace alone. However, the concept embraced God's just punishment of the wicked (which glorified God) and the cursing of the renegade and reprobate. Paul Garnet,* **Salvation and Atonement In The**

Dead Sea Scrolls (J. C. B. Mohr: Tubingen, 1977), p. 20. The central problem in Judaism was the relationship between grace and works. Grace was supplementary to works. It existed within the framework of the Law. Kittel and Friedrich, "charis," 9:388.

13. *Titus 2:9.*

14. *Acts 15:11.*

15. *Romans 3:21.*

16. *Ephesians 2:5.*

17. *Romans 5:8.*

18. *Romans 5:15-18; 6:23; Ephesians 2:8.*

19. *John 1:17.*

20. *Romans 5:1-2.*

21. *Ephesians 2:8-9.*

22. *Ephesians 2:10.*

23. *Matthew 19:29; 25:34; Mark 10:17; Luke 10:25; Acts 20:32; 26:18; 1 Corinthians 9:6; Galatians 5:21; Ephesians 1:11, 14; 5:5; Colossians 1:12; 1 Peter 1:3-4; Revelation 20:7.*

24. *Matthew 19:29.*

25. *Acts 16:28.*

26. *Ephesians 1:11.*

27. *Colossians 1:12.*

28. *1 Peter 1:3-4.*

29. *Acts 2:38; Gal. 3:26-27.*

30. *1 John 5:3; 2 John 6; John 14:15, 21, 23.*

31. *James 2:14-26.*

CHAPTER SEVEN
QUESTIONS

1. What two questions focus the conflict between Pharisaism and the gospel?

2. In the Pharisees' view, what made a Jew righteous?
   A. Righteousness was not the result of what?
   B. Righteousness was the result of what?

3. Discuss what Paul, the former Pharisee, said about righteousness in the following passages:
   A. Philippians 3:9
   B. Philippians 3:5-6.
   C. 1 Corinthians 1:30
   D. 2 Corinthians 5:21
   E. Romans 1:17
   F. Romans 3:21-22
   G. Romans 9:30-32

4. What did the Pharisees believe the relationship between obedience and grace was?

5. Discuss the parallel between the Pharisees' view of grace and many New Testament Christians' view.

6. What are the consequences of Christians believing obedience is the means of becoming righteous?

7. What do the following passages say about salvation by grace?
   A. Titus 2:9
   B. Acts 15:11
   C. Romans 3:21
   D. Ephesians 2:5
   E. John 1:17
   F. Romans 5:1-2

8. What does being saved by grace mean?

9. Explain the nature of the gift of an inheritance. Show clearly by the New Testament that salvation is an inheritance.

10. What are the three purposes of obedience?

THOUGHT QUESTION

Why is it crucial for a Christian to understand the meaning of salvation through faith by grace?

CHAPTER EIGHT

PHARISAISM: THE BINDING OF INTERPRETATIONS

Any religious body sincerely searching for truth is a thinking group of people. They study Scripture with an inquiring mind. They are open to examining all of Scripture's teachings from any valid perspective. As they study, they will conduct a dialogue among themselves and with others as they seek deeper insights and clearer understandings. Different perspectives will exist within the group itself. Those perspectives will be discussed openly and vigorously. There will be obvious, sincere disagreements. However, as long as the whole body knows and acknowledges it is seeking truth, there is no threat to sincere searchers in disagreement. The basic objective of any religious body in this situation is acquiring understanding. The object of study, questioning, and discussion-disagreement is to gain a more accurate understanding.

When such a religious body reaches the state that it is convinced it has unquestionably found the truth, a definite transformation begins. The members no longer search for better understandings; they begin defending accepted understandings. Truths which were found crystallize into fixed positions. There is no longer room for differing perspectives. Differing perspectives become evidence of false doctrine. Any serious disagreement threatens to rupture fellowship. Searching questions, questions which seek honest answers to legitimate "whys" are regarded as a sign of heresy or of faithlessness. Those who see flaws in accepted positions are considered dangerous persons who are seeking to lead the faithful astray. No longer is the objective to understand. The group acquires a new objective. The basic objective becomes imposing conformity on all members. Now one demonstrates faithfulness by accepting approved positions. The group feels threatened by a studying, inquiring mind who continues to search for understanding. The religious body is convinced that its survival is dependent upon binding its accepted interpretations on all within the group.

The Binding Pharisees

The Pharisees evolved from serious religious thinkers who wished to apply the law to the real issues and needs of the day. A seeking spirit searching for understanding inhabited the Pharisees' forefathers. In the formative beginning of the movement, they challenged accepted positions, asked valid questions, and looked from all valid perspectives.

In time, the Pharisees assumed the position of religioius authority. Their understandings became the commonly accepted positions. They declared that they properly represented the teachings of the law. The truth was reflected in their views. Thus, they became a religious sect of fixed positions which were stringently defended and staunchly bound on others.

The enormous tension which existed between Jesus and the Pharisees is evident is the gospels. That tension existed because Jesus' teaching demanded that the Pharisees rethink and reconsider some of their authoritative interpretations of the law. Jesus continually challenged them to think, to search, and to seek a more accurate understanding of the intent of the law. Jesus was not challenging them to doubt, but to deepen their insight and understanding. Jesus was not a threat to the law; he was a threat to fixed interpretations which missed the point of the law.

Since they regarded themselves and were accepted as religious authorities, they rejected Jesus' questions as honest inquiries. Instead, He and His teachings were considered a threat to their authoritative position as experts and to the validity of their interpretations of the law.

A Classic Example

Matthew 12:1-14 is a classic example of Jesus challenging the Pharisees' interpretation of the law. The heart of the issue was the proper observance of the Sabbath. As noted in chapter five, Exodus 20:8-11 prohibited work on the Sabbath. That was unquestionable divine law in the Mosaical code. However, there was no comprehensive definition of work in the Mosaical law or the Old Testament. To make the law obeyable, the Pharisees defined work in every conceivable context. This was an obvious necessity if people were to obey the law. Their definitions became the bound interpretation of how to keep the Sabbath properly. Their interpretations were law. Failure to abide by those interpretations was a serious spiritual infraction. In their thinking, Jesus' challenges to their fixed interpretations were challenges to divine truth.

The first incident centered in the disciples' conduct on a Sabbath. It was near the time of harvest. Jesus and the disciples were walking by a grain field. The Pharisees were following. The disciples, being hungry, stripped some of the ripe grain from the stalks and ate the raw grain. The Pharisees immediately charged the disciples with violating the Sabbath.

To understand the issue one must understand the source of contention. Both the Pharisees and Jesus agreed that certain circumstances made it permissible to work on the Sabbath. Jesus taught that it was permissible to care for human needs on the Sabbath. The Pharisees acknowledged that rescuing a domesticated animal from danger,[1] defending oneself against an attacking enemy,[2] and saving personal belongings from one's burning home[3] were permissible on the Sabbath. They both agreed that exceptions to the Sabbath law existed. However, the Pharisees did not regard the disciples' deed as permissible.

The Pharisees by their oral law had defined work by dividing it into 39 categories.[4] Two of those categories were reaping and threshing.[5] According to their oral law, the act of stripping the heads of grain was an act of reaping or threshing. By their fixed interpretation, it constituted an act of work and thereby violated the Sabbath.

Jesus challenged their position in three ways. First, he declared that their interpretation failed to account for all considerations. When David was fleeing from King Saul, he requested and received the showbread to be used for his own provision.[6] The law specified that this bread was for the priests alone.[7] Yet David was not condemned for taking and eating the bread. If David's eating showbread was not regarded as an act of sin, how could his disciples' eating raw grain be classified as sin? Second, Jesus noted that the priests in conducting their religious duties commonly worked on the Sabbath. Yet their acts of work were never regarded as violations of the Sabbath. Third, Jesus quoted from Hosea 6:6, "I desire mercy, and not sacrifice." He declared that if they had understood what Hosea meant, they would not have condemned the guiltless disciples. The disciples' hunger should have provoked sympathy rather than condemnation. In the Pharisees' dedication to the letter of the law, they had lost the heart of God.

Jesus could have cited other examples for further questioning of the Pharisees' fixed interpretation of violation of the Sabbath. When Israel crossed the Jordan and prepared to attack Jericho, God commanded Joshua to take the men of war and march around the city once for six days and seven times the seventh day.[8] One of those days was the Sabbath. That instruction was in violation of the accepted understanding of keeping the Sabbath. After the walls of Jerusalem were rebuilt following the return from Babylonian exile, the Jews were violating the Sabbath.[9] Foodstuffs were being transported into Jerusalem and sold. To end the violation, the gates of the city were closed on the Sabbath and guards were posted to prohibit entry.[10] The guards were working on the Sabbath to prohibit work on the Sabbath.

Jesus' challenge first declared that their definition of work was too narrow. It did not take into account all valid circumstances. Second, Jesus declared that people were God's primary concern. The law existed because of God's concern for the people. Mercy was more important than sacrifice because people were the focus of God's concern — not religious ordinances. Just as concern for people cannot set aside the law, neither can concern for the law ignore the valid needs of people.

The second incident also involved the question of working on the Sabbath. Jesus entered a synagogue. Present in the assembly was a man with a withered hand. Looking for a reason to accuse Jesus, the Pharisees asked him if it was lawful to heal on the Sabbath. Again, it is needful to understand the specific issue. The Pharisees had no objection to an act of healing on the Sabbath if a man's life was in immediate danger.[11] They did not regard saving a human life as a violation of the Sabbath. However, a withered hand was not a life-threatening condition. It could have been healed as easily on Sunday as on Saturday. Waiting until the Sabbath was over was an inconvenience, not jeopardy. To heal a man who was not in imminent danger was regarded as a violation of the Sabbath.

Jesus challenged the priorities established by their bound interpretation which defined work. He observed that anyone who had a sheep which fell into a pit on the Sabbath would rescue the sheep without hesitation. The oral law agreed that it was right to rescue the animal.[12] Jesus then declared the obvious: a man is more valuable than a sheep. If it is right to do good to a sheep on the Sabbath, it also must be right to do good to a man on the Sabbath. It was never in opposition to or violation of the law to do good on the Sabbath. The purpose of the Sabbath was not to discourage doing good by caring for existing human needs.

To underscore the truth of this position, Jesus healed the man. The challenge and the act of healing so angered the Pharisees that they began serious consideration of how to destroy Jesus.

The Issue

In both of these incidents, the issue was not the authority of the written law. Jesus and the Pharisees were in full agreement that the written law was authoritative. The issue was not the necessity of keeping the Sabbath day holy. Both agreed the Sabbath must be kept holy. The issue was not that work on the Sabbath violated the Sabbath. Both agreed work on the Sabbath was wrong.

In each incident the Pharisees' bound, inflexible definition of work was the issue. The Pharisees of themselves had decided what constituted a work violation of the Sabbath. Human judgments, not written Scripture, were the basis of their definitions. Jesus did not condemn their necessary use of human judgment in applying the law. Regarding their judgment as being equivalent to God's divine law was the source of the problem. Their human judgment, as all human judgment, involved some blind spots and basic inconsistencies. They lost sight of the fact that God was not interested in law for law's sake, but in law for people's sake. The law existed because of God's concern for His people. The law opposed sin, not good. If the law was used in opposition to doing good, the law was being used to oppose God's purposes and concerns. Their inflexible interpretations which they freely bound on others were not concerned with mercy. The God of mercy did not impose a law void of feeling on His people. The issue was their blind spots, their inconsistencies, and their failure to understand God's priority concerns and objectives. They could not see the flaws in their judgments (1) because their faith in their judgments was as devout as their faith in the written law, and (2) because their interpretations were regarded as being as valid and authoritative as the written law. In their eyes, Jesus was not challenging the fallibility of human judgment; Jesus was challenging God and His law.

If the Pharisees had seen Jesus' point, if they had acknowledged the need for better understanding, and if they had accepted responsibility for being flexible in their judgments, they would have become the most powerful and influential work force God has ever had on this earth. Because they refused to understand Jesus' concern about their emphasis and attitudes, they were Jesus' greatest obstacle in reaching the minds and hearts of the people.

All Christians need to learn from the Pharisees' mistake. All Christians are tempted strongly to bind their personal judgments and personal interpretations of Scripture upon others. It is extremely difficult to distinguish between personal judgment and divine teaching. Though difficult, one must make the distinction if faith is to rest on divine authority rather than on human opinion.

CHAPTER EIGHT
FOOTNOTES

1. *T. B. Shabbath 128b.*
2. *Josephus,* **Antiquities of the Jews,** *12.6.2.*
3. *M. Shabbath 16:2-4.*
4. *M. Shabbath 7:2.*
5. *M. Shabbath 7:2.*
6. *1 Samuel 21:1-6.*
7. *Leviticus 24:5-9.*
8. *Joshua 6:3-5.*
9. *Nehemiah 13:15-18.*
10. *Nehemiah 13:19-22.*
11. *M. Yoma 8:6-7.*
12. *T. B. Shabbath 128b.*

CHAPTER EIGHT
QUESTIONS

1. Discuss attitudes characteristic of a religious body searching for truth.
2. Discuss the changes which occur when that religious body is convinced it has found the truth.
3. Why did the tension exist between Jesus and the Pharisees? How did the Pharisees view the questioning Jesus?
4. Read Matthew 12:1-8.
   A. What did the disciples do?
   B. What was the Pharisees' charge?
   C. On what did Jesus and the Pharisees agree?

D. Discuss the three ways Jesus challenged their definition of work.
5. Read Matthew 12:9-14.
    A. What was the situation?
    B. When did the Pharisees regard an act of healing as a Sabbath violation?
    C. How did Jesus challenge their position?
    D. How did Jesus' act of healing affect the Pharisees?
6. What was not the issue? What was the issue?
7. What do Christians need to learn from the Pharisees' mistake?

THOUGHT QUESTION

Why is it hard for a Christian to distinguish between personal judgment and divine teaching?

NEW PHARISAISM: THE BINDING OF INTERPRETATIONS

In every generation the church has been properly concerned about protecting Christians from worldliness. The New Testament is quite specific about the spiritual consequence of loving the world. Injunctions against worldliness are explicit. John warned, "If any man love the world, the love of the father is not in him."[1] James stated there were two basic responsibilities inherent in having pure religion. The second was keeping oneself unspotted from the world.[2] He further declared, "Whosoever therefore would be a friend of the world maketh himself an enemy of God."[3] Paul stressed that a fundamental responsibility of basic Christian existence is to refuse to be fashioned according to this world.[4] The Christian, Demas, forsook the imprisoned Paul because he "loved this present world."[5] Devotion to or love of "the world" is a grave threat to spiritual existence.

Just as the Pharisees wanted to preserve the holiness of the Jews by protecting them from Sabbath violations, conscientious Christians want to preserve the holiness of God's people by protecting them from worldliness. Just as the Pharisees defined work in terms of current activities, Christians also have defined worldliness in terms of current activities. Just as the Pharisees bound their definitions on all Jews, Christians of each generation have bound their definitions of worldliness on other Christians.

Just as the Pharisees, Christians have determined faithfulness and the grounds of fellowship on the basis of their definitions. Christians are just as sensitive and defensive about their definitions as were the Pharisees. To challenge an accepted interpretation can produce as much resentment and hostility today as Jesus' challenges to the

73

Pharisees produced.

Defining Worldliness

Consider these illustrations of past bound definitions of worldliness. Prior to television, many declared that a Christian who attended any movie of any description was being worldly. Playing cards of any kind was regarded as worldly, and merely owning a deck of poker cards was worldly. Many regarded laughing, joking, and any form of merriment as worldly and unbecoming a Christian. The only godly frame of mind was somberness reflected in a dour face. Such interpretations of worldliness were held in absolute seriousness in a genuine desire to protect Christians.

A serious problem of modern Pharisaism exists in the Lord's church. It binds human judgments on other Christians by demanding conformity to accepted interpretations. Most of these interpretations come from sincere, genuine concern about the real problem of worldliness among God's people. However, New Testament Christians are in grave danger of ceasing to be the church governed by faith derived solely from knowledge of the Word. They are in danger of becoming a religious body dedicated to demanding comformity through acceptance of a modern oral law. Modern Pharisaism is the heart of much of the dissension, factions, and judgmental condemnations too commonly seen in the church.

The "back to the Bible" movement is moving further and further away from teaching people *why* Christians hold their ethical principles and moral values. Many hold the attitude that "why" is not important; the essential issue is that people conform to accepted standards. When New Testament Christians stop asking and understanding "why," the church will not remain long as the Lord's church. When one asks why certain standards are practiced by Christians, he rarely receives a Biblical explanation of morals and ethics. Instead, he is told, "Because it is right." "That is church of Christ teaching." "That is what the preacher (or elders) said." "That is what we have always done."

Such premises for determining Christian conduct would cause our great restoration leaders of the past to moan in disbelief. For generations simple New Testament Christianity has fought the binding of human authorities based on human judgments derived from selective use of Scripture. Ceaselessly, issue has been taken with denominational advocates who declared they did something "because it was right," "because that is what our church teaches," "because that is what the preacher says," "because that is what we have always done."

For generations New Testament Christians have groaned as they listened to religious advocates take proof-texts out of context to defend positions. Who could have believed the day would come when New Testament Christians used the same approach to determine proper Christian conduct?

Two pillars undergird the simple Christianity founded on Jesus and His authority. (1) It is necessary for every Christian to be a student of the Word in order to possess the faith produced by knowledge.[6] (2) Each Christian forever has the freedom and the responsibility to understand the Word and to base his life on that understanding. There is no individual or collective human head of the church who determines "the doctrine" or "the standards."

Two attitudes were indispensable to the restoration of New Testament Christianity in this country: (1) "Where the Bible speaks, we speak; where the Bible is silent, we are silent"; and (2) "In matters of faith — unity; in matters of opinion — liberty; in all things — love." In the interpretive judgments which are bound today, there is much speaking where the Bible does not speak. Commonly, there is too little love and no area of opinion today — human judgments are regarded as matters of faith.

An Example

Today in many congregations a man who does not drink, who does not smoke, who does not dance and forbids his family to dance, who forbids his wife and children to wear brief or tight apparel, and who faithfully attends the weekly assemblies is regarded as a model Christian of excellent influence. He is regarded as a devout Christian because his life conforms to accepted interpretations of proper Christian standards. This same man can love his possessions, be a materialist, be covetous, and be a "hardnosed" businessman who uses people to make money. These things will not affect his image as a model Christian. Were he to begin drinking, he would destroy his image; but his love of possessions disturbs no one. Were he to begin smoking, he would be tarnished; but his materialism troubles no one. Were he to allow his children to dance, his influence would suffer; but his covetousness is accepted without comment. Were his wife to begin wearing a bikini in public, he would be disgraced; but he can exploit people for business' sake with impunity. Drinking (not drunkenness), smoking, dancing, and wearing sensual apparel involve interpretations of Biblical principles. Loving possessions,[7] materialism,[8] covetousness,[9] and the financial exploitation of people[10] are clear and specific violations of plain scriptural teachings.

The point is not that drinking, smoking, dancing, and wearing sensual apparel are innocent, harmless, and pose no spiritual dangers. The question is this: how can the church's human judgment and interpretations be more important than explicit teachings of Scripture in determining faithfulness? How can one who rejects specific scriptural teaching be regarded faithful because he accepts established human judgments? Is the primary basis of faithfulness human judgments or the Word itself?

This is the precise situation that created the gulf between Jesus and the Pharisees. Jesus condemned them for the problem. In Matthew 23:23-24 Jesus did not condemn them for tithing mint, anise, and cummin, but for leaving undone the weightier matters of the law. He condemned them because they had meticulously strained out the gnat while they blindly swallowed the camel. One wonders if He passes the same judgment on His people today.

A Model Argument

Less than a generation ago the pulpit consistently condemned smoking. It was affirmed that smoking tobacco was an act of worldliness which could result in a person's eternal condemnation. While many Christians smoked, most Christians regarded smoking to be sinful. Many Christian smokers felt obligated to apologize for their habit. Many openly acknowledged, "I know this is wrong; I need to stop."

Rarely was smoking opposed on the basis of Christian ethics. It was opposed on the basis of a prooftext — 1 Corinthians 3:16-17:

> Know ye not that ye are the temple of God, and that the Spirit of God dwelleth in you? If any man destroyeth the temple of God, him shall God destroy; for the temple of God is holy, and such are ye.

This is the argument which declared smoking to be sinful. (1) The Christian's physical body is the temple of God. (2) God will destroy the person who destroys His holy temple. (3) Smoking can cause lung disease, heart disease, and cancer. (4) Thus smoking is a sin which will bring God's destruction on the person who destroys the temple.

There are two basic flaws with this modern oral law argument. The first flaw is that it takes 1 Corinthians 3:16-17 out of context. It is a fact that 1 Corinthians 6:19-20 taught that the Christian's body was the temple of the Holy Spirit. That passage condemned fornication which was declared to be a sin against a person's physical body (6:18). However, this was not the point of 3:16-17. Note in 3:16-17 that "ye" (plural) are "a" (ASV) or "the" (KJV) temple (literally, sanctuary) of

God. This passage was directed to the Corinthian congregation collectively. In this analogy, Paul said as a congregation they were the temple or sanctuary of God. Some within the congregation were about to destroy the church. Some were destroying it through internal division.[11] Others were destroying it by honoring the Greek philosophy of wisdom above the teachings of Christ.[12] Because Greek wisdom mocked the idea of a crucified and resurrected Savior,[13] some were ashamed to affirm salvation by the crucified, resurrected Jesus.[14] Many remained carnal babes who professed spiritual loyalty to human teachers.[15] These feelings, attitudes, and misunderstandings left uncorrected were destined to destroy the church in Corinth. All who endorsed such were involved in destroying God's sanctuary or temple in that city. Paul was emphasizing the seriousness of being a part of forces which threatened the destruction of the congregation. In this passage Paul was not speaking of the physical well-being of the human body but of the spiritual well-being of the church.

The second flaw is found in the fact that the argument is both limited and inconsistent. That was Jesus' precise objection to the Pharisees' argument in Matthew 12:3-7. The argument did not take into rightful consideration all relevant matters. For example, Jesus taught that if necessary, His disciple must sacrifice his life for faithfulness to Jesus.[16] In the first century many Christians endured physical persecution to the point of dying. Did their submission to the physical destruction of the body constitute an act of sin? Did they sin against Christ by obeying Christ? Compare these questions to those Jesus asked the Pharisees in Matthew 12:3-5.

Many things other than smoking can destroy the body. Overeating, overweight, and improper diet are major causes of bad health and death. Many people significantly shorten their lives by working too hard for too many hours at a stressful job, or by working in a highly hazardous job. Others destroy their health and shorten their lives by getting too little rest over a long period of time. Some fail to prevent serious health problems by getting too little exercise. Since each of these can also result in a shortened life, are they to be classified as sins? Would one be condemend and rejected by God as quickly for these as he would be for smoking?

The issue is this: are Christians to function as the Pharisees of today by labeling all matters as sin or good? Are they to go beyond clear teachings of Scripture, make new definitions and classifications of sin, and bind these definitions? Can Christian life and faithfulness to Jesus be reduced to compliance to formulated conduct based on human judgments which define righteous living?

Spiritual Soundess

Today spiritual soundness frequently is declared to be conformity to accepted standards. A Christian does not have to believe dancing is wrong, just do not dance. Understanding why drinking is spiritually dangerous is unnecessary; just do not drink. Regardless of what one believes or understands, he is "faithful" if he conforms. Knowledge of the Word, personal faith, and personal understanding have nothing to do with personal righteousness. Being righteous merely is doing the right things regardless of attitude, feelings, or convictions. That is NOT New Testament Christianity. Jesus stressed that a religious act was meaningless unless it was done for the right reason, for the right motive, and with the right attitude.[17] Proper motives and attitudes are never the product of ignorance or habit.

The Basic Premise of Christianity

The basic premise of New Testament Christianity is this: every Christian must have a personal faith in Christ. That faith can be built only on knowledge of the Word. That faith must be the basis of one's personal response to God in becoming a Christian, in acting as a Christian, in serving as a Christian, and in living as a Christian. Conforming to accepted regulations produced by human judgments does not make one a Christian. The expression of knowledgeable faith in the Lord makes one a Christian.

The pulpit and classroom must stop teaching people to conform and begin teaching them the Word. The Word is not taught by using select prooftexts to advocate human judgments. Christians need the whole Word taught in context. Righteousness must be advocated as earnestly as evil is resisted. Righteous living is not the mere absence of sins in one's life; it is the active practice of godly conduct and Christian service. Both are equally essential.

CHAPTER NINE
FOOTNOTES

1. *1 John 2:15b.*

2. *James 1:27.*

3. *James 4:4b.*

4. *Romans 12:2.*

5. *2 Timothy 4:10.*

6. *Romans 10:17.*
7. *Matthew 6:24.*
8. *1 Timothy 6:9-10.*
9. *Colossians 3:5-6.*
10. *James 5:4.*
11. *1 Corinthians 1:10-17.*
12. *1 Corinthians 1:18-25.*
13. *Acts 17:29-32.*
14. *1 Corinthians 1:26 — 2:5.*
15. *1 Corinthians 3:1-9.*
16. *Matthew 10:38-39; 16:24-25.*
17. *Matthew 6:1-18.*

CHAPTER NINE
QUESTIONS

1. Explain the parallel between Christians' desire to protect the church against worldliness and the Pharisees' desire to protect the Jews against Sabbath violations.

2. What are some of the former definitions of worldliness which were bound on the church in generations past?

3. What is the church in grave danger of becoming?
   A. If Christians stop asking "why," what will be the consequence?
   B. What are some unacceptable answers to proper questions of "why"?

4. What two pillars undergird simple Christianity?

5. What two attitudes are indispensable to the restoration of New Testament Christianity?

6. Explain how a person can become a model Christian through conformity to accepted interpretations while disregarding New Testament teachings.

7. Give the old argument which was used to condemn smoking.
   A. What are two basic flaws in that argument?
   B. In regard to such reasonings, what issue must be faced?

8. Explain this statement: "Frequently spiritual soundness is declared to be conformity to accepted standards."

9. What is the basic premise of Christian existence?

THOUGHT QUESTION

Why do many Christians prefer a religious life of conformity to a spiritual life of faith?

CHAPTER TEN

ETHICS RATHER THAN PHARISAISM

Determining right and wrong conduct is never simple. People who prefer wrongdoing rationalize it into acceptability. People preferring right conduct but who hold preconceptions are blind to all perspectives but their own. "Gray" areas of conduct which require thought, understanding, and accurate knowledge create problems for everyone.

For the person who accepts Jesus Christ as Lord and Scripture as God's revelation, some aspects of the problem are simplified. Some things are specifically declared to be wrong: lying, stealing, fornication, adultery, drunkenness, murder, etc. Some things are specifically declared to be right: obedience to Christ, holiness, purity, kindness, meekness, self-control, etc. It is never wrong to be holy, and it is never right to commit fornication.

Yet, revelation of absolutes does not resolve the issue. Revealed evils often are transformed into good by challenging definitions and appealing to circumstances. The plea is, "How can that be wrong in this circumstance?" Thus, danger makes lying good; necessity makes stealing good; love makes fornication good, etc. Appeal to circumstances also makes right conduct wrong. The plea is, "In these circumstances is it not hurtful to do what is right?" Thus, obedience is "showing off"; holiness is hypocrisy; purity is arrogance; self-control is snobbishness, etc.

In the "gray" areas where absolutes do not exist, moral anarchy often reigns. The problem of defining, identifying, and appropriately dealing with worldliness is one such area.

Proper Behavior

Two basic ways are used to determine and to regulate godly

behavior. The first can be called "rule" behavior. Proper "rules" which must be respected are composed and authoritatively declared. They are the regulatory authority over one's actions. It is imperative to know and keep the rules. The rules are to be accepted, never questioned. If one regulates his conduct by the right rules, he is said to be a godly person.

Rule behavior is programmed behavior. One does not think; he reacts to the situation. His life is programmed by rules for specific reactions regardless of real needs, legitimate questions, or conditions. Rule behavior is the essence of Pharisaism.

The second is moral behavior based on Christian ethics. One understands basic Christian principles. When applied principles serve as spiritual guidelines, one is godly. One's actions are determined by (1) knowledge of the principles, (2) understanding the principles, (3) making decisions on the basis of the principles, and (4) determining conduct by applying the principles. Ethical behavior is based on thought and understanding. It is the essence of Christian conduct.

Christian Ethics

Ethics is the study of that which is right and good, right conduct and the good life. Its objective is to determine what is right or good in distinction to that which is wrong or bad. It seeks to answer the questions, "What am I to do? How am I to act? What is proper conduct?"

Morality is the practice of that which one believes to be right or good. Morality applies ethics to daily life.

Christian ethics is but one of many forms of theological ethics. All religions have a system of ethics: Judaism, Islam, Buddhism, etc. The teachings of Jesus and revelations of the Word are the basis of Christian ethics.

New Testament writings are founded on ethical principles. Most of the epistles instructed Christians in ethical concepts. These writings explained what Christians were to do. Ask, "What should a Christian do about personal spiritual standards? about obeying the government? about association with weaker Christians?" Read Romans 12-15. This was an ethics-based response to those questions. 1 Corinthians declared to Corinthian Christians what to do regarding fornication in the church,[1] lawsuits between Christians,[2] sacrifices to idols,[3] and the proper use of spiritual gifts.[4] 1 Peter instructed those Christians about what to do in the face of physical persecution.[5] These were not lists of rules and regulations. They were explanations of proper conduct founded on Christian principles. They were challenges to understand the reasons for such conduct.

Ask, "What were they to do?" and read any epistle. The use of Christian principles in explaining proper Christian conduct clearly will be evident. That is Christian ethics.

Basic Christian Principles

There are basic Christian principles which govern a Christian's life at all times under all circumstances. The significance of these principles is rooted in the Lordship of Jesus and His atoning, reconciling sacrifice. Never is there a time or a circumstance when these principles are not relevant to a Christian's life and conduct. An entire book could be written about each. Following is a brief description of four principles.

Principle one is holiness. 1 Peter 1:13-16 declares that it is imperative for a Christian to be holy. Without holiness, one cannot be the living sacrifice.[6] Before Jesus' birth, God had decided that people who would be holy would be His people.[7] Jesus effected reconciliation between God and man to present the Christian holy and without blemish before God.[8]

The primary meaning of the Greek word *hagios* (holy) is separate or set apart. The Christian has been set apart from sin through the blood of Jesus to exist exclusively for God's use and service. He was a part of the kingdom of darkness but now is a citizen in the kingdom of light.[9] The Christian will live and act at all times as a person set apart for God.

Principle two is purity. The Greek words translated pure (*hagnos* and *katharos*) signified moral purity and cleanness. Jesus stressed that purity originated within, from the heart.[10] He renounced the ritual purity of the Pharisees which stresses external appearances.[11] If one belongs to Christ, he will be pure in heart,[12] will be unspotted from the world,[13] will refuse to partake of others' sins,[14] and will accept Jesus alone as his standard of purity.[15]

Principle three is righteousness. The Greek word *dikaios* (righteous) had broad usage. It signified a just person who treated God and people fairly. It signified a person whose life and actions submitted to and conformed to the will of God. An understanding of Romans 3 is essential to a proper understanding of Christian righteousness. A Christian cannot achieve righteousness through human deeds. He becomes righteous through the faith which enables him to receive atonement and justification.[16] Having been made righteous by God through Jesus, he accepts the responsibility of living and acting like a righteous person.

Principle four is agape love, the foundation ethic of Christian conduct. The verb and noun forms of *agape* are found over 250 times in the New Testament. It is the love of John 3:16, Matthew 22:37-39, John 14:15, Galatians 2:20, and 1 Corinthians 13. Romans 13:8 declared it to be the continuing Christian indebtedness. *Agape* love is not founded on emotion. It comes from the mind and is founded on the will. It seeks the highest of God and of people. Its sole concern is for that which is in God's best interest and in people's best interest (mate, child, neighbor, or enemy).

Ethical Questions

When a Christian approaches any decision or develops his lifestyle, he must ask questions which honor these principles. His understanding of the principles will determine his decisions and conduct.

"Will this allow me to exist as a person set apart for Christ? Is it consistent with a life set apart for God's service? Will it be evident to sinners and Christians that I am set apart? Will I appear to have the mind and heart of those who do not belong to Christ?"

"Will this allow me to be morally pure and clean? Will it reflect the appearance of a morally upright person? Will it compromise my purity by making it appear to be shallow or an external facade? Will I appear to have an unclean or impure mind and heart? Will it give outward evidence of the spiritual person I am inwardly? Is it consistent with the standards and attitude of purity of Jesus my Lord?"

"Will I be treating God fairly if I act or live this way? Will it allow me to give fair treatment to my family, my neighbors, my fellow Christians, or people about me? Will anyone suffer injustice as a result of this? Will it encourage or resist the will of God in my life? Will it allow me to be perceived as the righteous person Jesus Christ made me? Will it elevate or debase righteousness within me?"

"Does this seek God's highest good in my life? Does it seek the highest good of people about me? Will it encourage selfishness or promote a deepening awareness of and concern for God and for others? Will this promote the attributes and attitude of *agape* clearly set forth in 1 Corinthians 13?"

Ethics and Worldliness

The last chapter raised some questions about areas defined to be worldly by Pharisaic rules: smoking, drinking, dancing, and wearing sensual apparel. How can these areas be approached and considered on an ethical basis?

The questions which seek to apply Christian principles to conduct are relevant. Consider smoking in the light of these principles. One needs to ask if this habit affects his spiritual image in the eyes of others. "Am I seen as a spiritual person who exercises self-control, or am I seen as an undisciplined person ruled by habit?"

Overwhelming evidence documents the fact that smoking tobacco significantly contributes to heart disease, lung cancer, emphysema, and other disabling diseases. Every Christian represents a major investment made by God. There is nothing God and our Lord Jesus need more on this earth than the manpower and faithful influence of devout Christians. The Lord needs every faithful Christian for as many years as possible helping to support and to achieve the work of the church. There are so few Christians and such enormous needs. If a Christian smokes, and if smoking cuts short his or her service as a result of ill health or an early death, has he or she been fair to God? Has he or she been fair to those who would have profited from his or her continued spiritual work? Considering the enormous investment God and Jesus made in that person, does an unncessarily shortened life grant them a just return on that investment? Would a shortened life be in the highest interest of God and Christ?

When a Christian sees a serving, worshipping, sacrificial Christian of beautiful godly character dying unnecessarily early due to heart disease, lung cancer, or emphysema induced by smoking, the loss seems bitterly unnecessary. Faithful fellow Christians often feel robbed because a mature spiritual warrior has been lost.

In regard to drinking, it is unquestionable that drunkenness is a sin.[17] The first danger associated with drinking is identifying the point of drunkenness. Few can define that boundary for themselves.

What about drinking which does not become drunkenness? In the American culture, there are relevant ethical questions to be asked. "Does my drinking allow me to exist as a person set apart for Christ in the eyes of sinners and of Christians? Does it help establish or contribute to my spiritual cleanness and uprightness? Does it allow me to treat God fairly in proper utilizaiton of my influence as His child? Does it result in just representation of fellow Christians? Does it lead me to a greater dependence on God's will? Does it create circumstances or cultivate influences which rival or oppose God's will and influence in my life? Is it a practice which encourages me to seek the highest good of God and my fellow Christians? Will it produce the type of influence which allows me to seek the highest good of the lost?"

Combatting the problem of worldliness which is expressed through sensual lusts always has been a difficult problem. First, it must be understood that sexual drives of themselves are not sinful. Human sexual natures were God-given and God-designed from the moment of creation.[18] Sexual intimacy, fulfillment, and pleasure within marriage is godly, good, and wholesome.[19] The abuse of the sexual desire outside of marriage is sinful.

For years Christians have tried to regulate the problem of sensual lusts by imposing rules and regulations. The rules have been numerous. Do not dance. Do not wear clothing shorter than "X" inches or lower than "X" point. Do not attend R- or X-rated movies. Do not engage in mixed swimming, attend floor shows, or attend entertainment featuring striptease artists. For two reasons the rule approach has been woefully ineffective. First, those who kept or broke the rules rarely understood the real problem. Second, Christians found numerous other means not regulated by the rules to indulge their lusts.

As an illustration, consider the question of appropriate dress for a Christian woman. Rules which declare the length of the hemline or the height of the neckline are inadequate or ineffective. A woman can dress sensually and create a "sexy" appearance in many ways other than wearing revealing clothing. The tightness of a garment, the emphasis of a garment, or the sheerness of a garment can generate sensuality as easily as can the brevity of a garment.

Neither can a few places be designated as "off-limits" to men and thereby eliminate the opportunity for enticement. The opportunities for looking lustfully at a woman, a woman who seeks to entice and to generate sexual attraction, exist everywhere every day.

It is impossible for rules to regulate or to eliminate the problem of sensual lusts. One can devise the strictest set of rules imaginable, and still abundant opportunity will exist to indulge one's lusts without breaking the rules.

Jesus declared if a man looked upon a woman to lust after her he was guilty of sexual sin.[20] Obviously, if a woman acts or dresses in an overt, knowing manner to entice a man to lust for her (outside of marriage), she becomes a participant in his sin by deliberately provoking him to sin.

The only solution to the problem of lust is a spiritual individual accepting the responsibility to regulate his or her conduct and habits on a clear understanding of Christian principles. Again, ethical questions must be asked and answered, "Do I look like a person set apart for Christ, or do I look like a person enhancing sex appeal to generate a sensual appearance? Am I dressed like a godly person of Christian character, or as a sex object? Am I trying to make my Christian character evident, or am I trying to boost my ego by displaying my body? Do I attract people's attention because of the person I am or because of the body and physique I display? Are my scents, my mannerisms, and my appearance designed to cause others to see me as sexually desirable in a deliberate effort to appeal to their sensual feelings? If I am acting, talking, or dressing in a manner to appeal to others' lusts, am I seeking their highest interests? Am I seeking God's highest interests in my life? If I am exploiting others' sexual emotions, am I treating them justly, fairly? Will they view me as a clean, morally pure person, or will they believe I share their sexual fantasies and lustful desires? Am I encouraging myself to develop a deeper sense of godliness, or am I encouraging sensual feelings which work in opposition to godliness?"

Such ethical concerns will cause any devout Christian to view all forms of entertainment which generate pleasure by appealing to sexual passion (dancing, movies, live shows) from a new perspective. It will cause him or her to view clothing, conversational language and subjects, actions, and mannerisms from a new perspective. Only a godly perspective in the individual Christian's mind can fight the problem effectively.

The Bottom Line

Combatting worldliness in any form is primarily an individual fight. Worldliness will never be legislated out of the lives of Christians through declared rules demanding conformity. The war will be fought effectively and won only if Christians are taught and will understand Christian principles.

Every Christian will not answer ethical questions in the same way. Differing levels of spiritual knowledge and maturity often will result in different answers. The New Testament teaches there are areas regulated by conscience, and individual decisions in such areas must be respected.[21] However, areas of conscience are not the license selfishly to indulge the flesh. Ultimately, each Christian will explain his or her standards and deeds to the Lord. Each will give an account of his or her fidelity to holiness, purity, righteousness, and *agape* love.

Many Christians do not like the ethical approach because it requires knowledge and understanding which produce greater personal responsibility. They prefer easily applied rules based on others' knowledge and understanding. However, Christianity is a way of life which begins in the mind and heart. It cannot exist in shallow rules which regulate the body.

This fact has been obvious from Christianity's beginning: the greater the spiritual maturity of the individual, the more stringent and conscientious the personal application of the principles of holiness, purity, righteousness, and *agape* love.

CHAPTER TEN
FOOTNOTES

1. *1 Corinthians 5.*
2. *1 Corinthians 6:1-11.*
3. *1 Corinthians 8.*
4. *1 Corinthians 12-14.*
5. *1 Peter 3:13 — 4:19.*
6. *Romans 12:1-2.*
7. *Ephesians 1:3-4.*
8. *Colossians 1:21-22.*
9. *Colossians 1:11-12.*
10. *Matthew 15:10-20.*
11. *Matthew 23:25-28.*
12. *Matthew 5:8.*
13. *James 1:27.*
14. *1 Timothy 5:22.*
15. *1 John 3:2-3.*
16. *Romans 3:21-26.*
17. *Romans 13:13; 1 Corinthians 5:11; 6:10; Galatians 5:21; Ephesians 5:18.*
18. *Genesis 1:27-28.*
19. *1 Corinthians 7:3-5; Hebrews 13:4.*
20. *Matthew 5:28.*
21. *Romans 14; 1 Corinthians 8; Colossians 2:16-23.*

CHAPTER TEN
QUESTIONS

1. Explain why determining right or wrong conduct will never be a simple matter.

2. What are the two basic approaches to determining and regulating godly behavior?
   A. Explain rule behavior.
   B. Explain moral behavior.
   C. How do the two differ?

3. Define the words ethics and morality. Use Romans 12-15 to illustrate the fact that New Testament writings are founded on ethical principles.

4. List and explain the four basic principles which are to govern a Christian's life.

5. What are some of the ethical questions which a Christian can ask when seeking to determine proper conduct?
   A. How can such questions be applied to smoking?
   B. How can they be applied to drinking?
   C. How can they be applied to dancing?
   D. How can they be applied to wearing sensual apparel?

6. Why is it impossible to legislate worldliness out of the lives of Christians by demanding conformity to rules?

7. Will all Christians answer ethical questions in the same way? Explain your answer.

THOUGHT QUESTION

Why is it difficult to respect another Christian's conscience when he is doing something you have decided it is wrong for you to do?

CHAPTER ELEVEN

PHARISAISM: HUMAN REASONING VERSUS REVELATION

The Pharisees were devoted to reason. Josephus said of the Pharisees, "They follow the conduct of reason; and what that prescribes to them as good for them, they do; and they think they ought earnestly to strive to observe reason's dictates for practice."[1] They devoutly believed that God used reason to guide men in their deliberations and to reveal to them the secrets of His law.[2] They considered it inconceivable that God could give laws which contradicted reason.[3] Their attitude toward the *lex talionis,* "an eye for an eye, and a tooth for a tooth," is an example of their devotion to reason. Because the law was regarded by them as an outrage to the conscience, reason demanded that it not be taken literally. They thus interpreted the law as meaning that monetary compensation must be given in such offenses.[4]

The Pharisees are not to be condemned for their devotion to reasoning. Application of Scripture is impossible without the use of sound reasoning. The Pharisees' mistake is found in the fact that at times they allowed reasoned conclusions to set aside divine truth.

A Classic Example

The confrontation the Pharisees initiated with Jesus in Matthew 15:1-20 is a classic example of the use of fallacious reasoning to set aside truth. The Pharisees challenged Jesus' position as a teacher from God by questioning His religious authority. They challenged Him to explain why He refused to honor the tradition of the elders by permitting His disciples to eat with unwashed hands. He was being accused of failing to respect proper religious authority.

Their question had nothing to do with hygiene. The issue was the accepted practice of the religious act of ceremonial washing which produced ritual purity. Ceremonial washing for the purification of the priests was required by the Torah.[5] There were also other instances of ritual washings for the sake of religious purity.[6]

The oral law prescribed necessary washings as a religious act prior to eating a meal.[7] Those regulations meticulously declared such details as the amount of water to be used, the manner of the double rinsing, things which contaminated the hands, how much of the hands were to be covered by the rinsing, and the kind of water to be used.[8] The Pharisees were so strict about these ordinances that they would not eat unless there was sufficient water available for proper ritual washing.[9]

The failure of Jesus' disciples to observe this ordinance was regarded by the Pharisees as a serious transgression of the truth. It was an open, inexcusable rejection of proper religious authority. However, this ordinance was not based on any Mosaical command or any Scripture. The custom's origin is unknown.[10]

A Flaw in Traditional Authority

Jesus did not deny the charge of transgressing the tradition of the fathers. He did not seek to defend the disciples. Rather, He addressed the heart of the issue by pointing to a serious flaw in traditional authority. He declared that their reasoned conclusions expressed through ordinances of the oral law at times literally transgressed revealed divine authority.

The ten commandments declared, "Honor thy father and mother."[11] While the law did not give a comprehensive definition of honoring, Jesus acknowledged the accepted understanding: honoring included respecting parents[12] and supporting parents who were in need.

The law also sanctioned the giving of gifts to the Jewish sanctuary. The tabernacle was built from such gifts.[13] All sacrifices and tithes were to be brought to the sanctuary/temple.[14] Moses instituted a tax to be paid by all, rich and poor, as atonement money which was to be used for the tabernacle.[15] Joash instituted the practice of placing a chest before the temple to collect contributions.[16] Malachi condemned the people for failing to contribute properly to the temple.[17] In the first century, treasury boxes were located in the Court of the Women for collecting contributions to the temple.[18]

These two expectations created an obvious possibility for conflict between two religious financial responsibilities. What must one do if he had vowed to give or had given a gift to the temple, and afterwards his parents sought his financial aid?

The Pharisees' method of reasoning regarding a conflict between honoring parents and giving a gift to the temple is not recorded. The conclusion they reached indicates their reasoning possibly followed these lines. (1) A vow cannot be broken.[19] If one vowed a gift to the temple, that vow must be kept. (2) The temple is God's presence in Israel.[20] Nothing superceded the importance of the temple. (3) Honoring God the Creator is more important than honoring man the created. Therefore, a person who had given a gift or pledged a gift to the temple could say to his needy parents, "That which I would have used to help you has been given to the temple." He thereby was absolved of responsibility to his parents. This was their reasoned conclusion.

There was one horrible flaw in that conclusion. Their reasoned conclusion rejected one of the ten commandments. Those commandments were the heart and core of the Mosaical law. Their reasoning expressed through traditional authority disregarded specific revelation. It literally voided God's Word. Their reasoned conclusion did not coincide with God's priorities.

Jesus declared this attitude and action to be hypocrisy. With such thinking they became the living fulfillment of Isaiah's prophecy.[21] They honored God with words while their hearts were far removed from God. Their worship became vanity because they founded their teachings on human concepts rather than on divine revelation.

True Purity

Jesus' defense of His disciples emphasized internal purity. He rejected the concept of ritual purity. Ceremonial deeds of the body which emphasized outward conditions and appearances did not purify. The purity of godliness came inwardly from the heart. It was evidenced by thoughts and attitudes expressed in words and deeds. Since evil also originated in the heart, defilement was an internal problem, not an external problem.

The disciples themselves did not understand Jesus' point. They questioned Jesus in the Pharisees' behalf declaring the Pharisees were offended. Jesus had to explain the point and the meaning of His reply to His own disciples. Not even to the Twelve was the truth self-evident.

Human Reasoning and Logic

Religious, reasoned conclusions commonly declare themselves to be logical deductions. The proper use of logic is an invaluable tool in determining truth. Logic, which is the science of proof, is concerned about the adequacy of evidences which are based on human reasoning. In logic's examination of evidences, it has a two-fold thrust. It seeks to verify truths by utilizing sound reasoning. It seeks to expose reasoning fallacies based on arguments containing unjustified inferences or mistaken implications.

Jesus and the writers of the New Testament made use of logic in defending or in presenting truth. Jesus' profound answer to the seemingly impossible question concerning taxes was a logical conclusion: give to Caesar that which belongs to Caesar, and give to God that which belongs to God.[22] In Galatians Paul effectively used logic to prove his teachings came by revelation from Jesus.[23] Hebrews uses a wealth of information to conclude logically that Jesus Christ is the only avenue to God's acceptance.

While logic is an effective tool to help determine truth, fallacious reasoning masquerading as logic is a destructive enemy of truth. Fallacious reasoning which pretends to be logic long has been a favored method of obscuring truth, denying truth, and presenting error as truth. Tragically, much of the religious reasoning which claims to be logical thinking is fallacious reasoning in cunning disguise.[24]

Logic and Divine Truth

Great care must be taken in using logic to determine divine truth. (1) One must understand common forms of fallacious reasonings which produce erroneous conclusions. (2) One must be well informed in Scripture itself. (3) One must have an accurate awareness of God's values, concepts, and standards. The logical process is destroyed by fallacious reasoning, by ignorance of Scripture, and by substituting human values, concepts, and standards for the divine.

Human comprehension of God, of divine principles, of divine values, and of eternal truths is limited to God's revelation through His Word. The Word completely reveals the *will* of God for man.[25] Knowledge regarding how people relate to God through Christ and regarding the life God desires of His people is complete. However, the Word does not reveal the complete *mind* of God. Paul declared, "O the depth of the riches of both the wisdom and knowledge of God! how unsearchable are his judgments, and his ways past tracing out! For who hath known the mind of the Lord? or who hath been his counselor?"[26] The finite human mind is not capable of comprehending the full mind of God. To declare that all thoughts, values, and understandings of God must be confined to the conclusions derived by the human mind is itself illogical.

This does not mean one should go beyond the revelation of the Word in determining the will of God. To do such is to substitute human speculation for truth revealed through the Holy Spirit. Never should anyone conclude that human judgments perceive God's thoughts, perspectives, values, and priorities more perfectly than Scripture's revelation of God's mind.

Because the human mind cannot comprehend fully the divine mind, great care must be exercised to be certain that reasoned conclusions do not contradict revealed truth. It is simple and convenient for reasoned conclusions to set aside divine truth. The Pharisees bear ancient testimony to that fact.

CHAPTER ELEVEN
FOOTNOTES

1. *Josephus,* **Antiquties of the Jews,** *18.1.3.*

2. *Umen, p. 23.*

3. *Ibid.*

4. *Ibid.*

5. *Exodus 30:18ff; Leviticus 15:1ff.*

6. *Exodus 19:10,14; 2 Samuel 12:20.*

7. *M. Berakoth 8:2-4.*

8. *M. Yadaim 2:1-4.*

9. *Mark 7:3-4.*

10. *Jack P. Lewis,* **The Gospel According to Matthew, Part II** *(Sweet Publishing Company: Austin, Texas, 1976), p. 23.*

11. *Exodus 20:12; Deuteronomy 5:16.*

12. *Exodus 21:17.*

13. *Exodus 35.*

14. *Deuteronomy 12:5-6.*

15. *Exodus 30:11-16.*

16. *2 Chronicles 24:8-14.*

17. *Malachi 3:8-12.*

18. *Luke 21:1-4.*

19. *Numbers 30:2.*

20. *1 Kings 8:10-13.*

21. *Isaiah 29:13.*

22. *Matthew 22:19-21.*

23. *Galatians 1:11-2:21.*

24. *Arlie Hoover's* **Don't You Believe It** (Moody Press: Chicago, 1982) is an enjoyable introduction to forms of fallacious reasoning which are commonly mistaken for logic.

25. *John 14:25; 16:13; 2 Timothy 3:16-17.*

26. *Romans 11:33-34.*

CHAPTER ELEVEN
QUESTIONS

1. Give evidence of the fact that the Pharisees were devoted to reason.

2. What was the significance of the Jewish practice of washing one's hands before eating?

3. The Pharisees regarded the disciples' failure to wash their hands before eating as what?

4. What serious flaw did Jesus reveal regarding the Pharisees' reasoned conclusions?
    A. What conflict could arise in Jewish obedience to the commandment, "Honor thy father and mother"?
    B. What was the Pharisees' reasoned conclusion regarding that possible conflict?
    C. What was the ultimate result of that reasoned conclusion?

5. What did Jesus stress in His defense of the disciples?

6. What is logic?
    A. What is the two-fold thrust of logic?
    B. Is it proper to use logic to determine spiritual truth? Explain your answer.

7. What is fallacious reasoning? Why is it dangerous?

8. What precautions must be taken when one uses logic to determine divine truth?

9. Discuss the human limitations in comprehending the mind of God.
   A. What do 2 Timothy 3:16-17, John 14:25, and John 16:13 state about the will of God for man?
   B. Why must one not go beyond the revelation of the Word in determining the will of God?

THOUGHT QUESTION

Why is the substitution of reasoned conclusions for revealed principles a common problem among Christians? Give some examples of the use of fallacious reasoning to set aside revealed truth.

CHAPTER TWELVE

NEW PHARASAISM: HUMAN REASONING VERSUS REVELATION

Reasoning has played an important role in the American restoration movement. "Come now, and let us reason together . . ."[1] has been the plea of restoration preachers for generations. The basic premise of the movement has been that all doctrines and spiritual practices bound on believers must be based on scriptural authority. For many years it was said that Scripture expresses its authority in three forms: a commandment, an example, or a necessary inference. In many instances, reasoning determined when an example was authoritative. Reasoning always determined when a necessary inference was authoritative.

With deeper study, it became apparent that those perceptions of scriptural authority were flawed. First, a command is unquestionably authoritative. However, there are comparatively few direct commands in the New Testament. Most instruction is based on principles to be understood and applied. Second, appeals to authoritative examples often involved subjective determinations. Distinguishing between binding and non-binding examples is often arbitrary. One Christian's binding example is another Christian's non-binding example. Third, appeals to necessary inference commonly involve subjective determinations. Using the same passages, Christians holding differing perspectives can and have reasoned themselves to conflicting necessary inferences. Often ignorance of first-century Jewish customs and of New Testament times results in faulty conclusions.

To illustrate the problem, consider the question, "How does the church properly conclude a worship assembly?" There is no specific teaching in the New Testament concerning the manner in which to conclude the worship assembly of the church. Yet, some have felt compelled to determine according to the authority of Scripture the "right" way to end a worship assembly. They noted that on the last night of Jesus' life when He instituted the Lord's Supper the gathering concluded by their singing a hymn and going out.[2] Even though the church had not been established at that time, even though the Christian age had not yet begun, and even though that was not a Christian worship assembly, they still reasoned that this was a binding example of how a worship assembly of the church should conclude. They failed to note that the institution of the Lord's Supper occurred during the observance of the Jewish Passover.[3] The Passover observance concluded with the singing of a hymn.[4] They thus bound a Passover practice on Christian worship.

The Problem of Silence

The New Testament is silent to an amazing degree in regard to a number of Christian practices in the first century. Consider again the worship assemblies of Christians. It is clearly evident that the Christians of the New Testament were devout worshippers.[5] Yet, there is little specific information in regard to the acts or the order of congregational worship in the first century. The fact that they sang, prayed, communed, were taught, and contributed in worship is clearly established. How they conducted those acts and in what order they conducted those acts is unknown. Not one single description of a Christian worship assembly is recorded in the New Testament. The closest the New Testament comes to giving such a description is Paul's discussion of inappropriate conduct in worship in 1 Corinthians 11 and 14. The earliest descriptions of Christian worship come from Pliny (a non-Christian writer who wrote ca. 110), Justin Martyr (ca. 150), Clement of Alexandria (ca. 190), and Tertullian (ca. 200).[6]

From silence, meager New Testament information, and reasoning, many Christians have formulated fixed worship practices which are regarded as bearing the stamp of scriptural authority. Some are so devout in their belief that these practices represent the Biblical order of Christian worship that they regard any deviations as conclusive evidence of congregational unfaithfulness or liberalism. In many instances these "divinely approved" ways to "scripturally" sing, pray, commune, be taught, and contribute are solely fashioned from reason and silence. In those instances reasoned conclusions formulate unbreakable laws.

Consider two examples of such reasoned ordinances. The first example is the ordinance of the use of invitation songs. This ordinance declares that every assembly, whether for worship or study, must conclude by extending an invitation to the lost through the singing of an invitation song. To exclude the invitation song is a digressive, liberal practice which rejects scriptural authority. It is reasoned that (1) Christ came to save the world; (2) congregations must be evangelistic; (3) the lost must be sought on every occasion; therefore, (4) the lost must be invited to Christ at every assembly.

Certainly, there is nothing wrong in using invitation songs or in inviting the lost to respond to Christ. However, one wonders when it was determined that the evangelistic thrust of a congregation in its community was fulfilled through singing an invitation song to a Christian assembly. There are even those who have concluded that unless a person responds during the invitation song his conversion is suspect. If Phillip had been of that persuasion, the Ethiopian eunuch would have faced a difficult situation.[7]

While there is nothing unscriptural about the practice, neither is the practice based on instruction from Scriptures which concern Christian worship. There is no teaching in the New Testament about invitation songs. There is no reference to that practice in first-century congregations. The general context of the epistles suggests worship assemblies were a time for God's spiritual family to praise the Lord and to be exhorted to godly living. Evangelism was a daily activity conducted privately and publicly from homes to synagogues to market places. Since there is no New Testament reference to the use of invitation songs, how can that practice be a matter of scriptural authority?

The second example is the ordinance of a united assembly. The ordinance declares that a congregation must gather the entire body of Christians in a single room for public worship. If the congregation is not physically present in one place at the same time, the worship is unscriptural. Any division of the worship assembly is a violation of the New Testament order of worship. Large congregations who have multiple assemblies are condemned. Congregations having special assemblies for children bussed to worship are in error. Such arrangements are "liberal" practices which exceed authority of Scripture. This reasoned conclusion appeals to 1 Corinthians 14:23 which discussed the importance of orderly conduct when "the whole church be assembled together" at Corinth. The specific subject of discussion in the passage was the abuse of spiritual gifts.

The Key Definition

One of the urgent emphases of the American restoration movement has been the autonomy of the local congregation. Many of the problems which precipitated the restoration movement were created by the control of a hierarchy over congregations in an area. Denominational hierarchies demanded their preachers conform to denominational doctrine rather than being devoted to Biblical teachings. Those hierarchies determined and bound doctrines and practices on their congregations. These two denominational practices helped created the mandate in the restoration movement for congregational autonomy. As the restoration movement matured, Christians realized the key to the existence of the New Testament church is found in the freedom and the life of a local congregation. Congregations in the New Testament were led by local leaderships.[8]

Scripture says little about relationships between congregations in the first century. It clearly documents that there were areas of cooperation,[9] but there is little specific information about the nature of that cooperation. Today out of concern for autonomy there are numerous unwritten ordinances which exist to regulate congregational cooperation in a manner which will guarantee the preservation of autonomy. It is obvious that the American restoration church has a concern for autonomy which is not paralleled in the New Testament because it confronts a problem which did not exist in the first century. It is equally obvious that today's ordinances concerning autonomy are a frequent source of problems.

To define and to preserve autonomy, one must define "a congregation." Perhaps the most critical definition made in the church today is the definition of "a congregaton." The accepted definition of today is a reasoned conclusion. From that reasoned conclusion have arisen some stringent laws about "a congregation," laws which often produce hurt and division. Those laws are the spirit and essence of the divisive anti-cooperation movement. They are the emotional flames of many brotherhood confrontations. They legislate a thousand matters about which Scripture is silent.

What is a congregation? Everyone knows the definition of a congregation. It is a body of Christians who meet in a specific building at a specific address. Ironically, the most critical definition to affect the life and work of a body of Christians in a community is based on a building. Everything about a local congregation is centered in its building: its membership, its leadership, its work, its finances, and its autonomy. Thus when Christians who assemble at one building interact too closely with Christians who assemble in another building, autonomy is violated and scriptural authority is exceeded. This definition of a congregation and the conclusions which accompany the definition are the product of reasoning and deductions. That reasoning and those deductions often ignore some of Scripture's evidences.

First, congregations definitely existed in the first century, but church buildings did not. There is no scriptural or historical evidence that any first-century congregation built, owned, or utilized a single building for worship assemblies. How then can a building be the basis of defining a congregation?

Second, some congregations were of such size that they exceeded the capacity of any known building in their area to house a single assembly of that congregation. The church at Jerusalem is always called "the church," never "the churches of Jerusalem" or "the congregations of Jerusalem." The "church" in Jerusalem had "elders," one congregation and one eldership.[10] It began with about 3,000 members.[11] That number grew daily.[12] Soon the number of men was about 5,000.[13] Later, "Believers were the more added to the Lord, multitudes of both men and women."[14] Still later the number of disciples multiplied exceedingly and included many priests.[15] How many thousand Christians were there in that one congregation?

The Jerusalem church owned no building. No known Jerusalem structure could house it in a single assembly. Early they assembled in the temple courtyard[16] which was likely the only area able to accommodate so many. However, that was a daily assembly, not the "worship" assembly. At an elevation of 2,000 feet, that open courtyard was subject to the wind, cold, rain, and occasional snow of a Jerusalem winter. That is an unlikely environment for worship in the winter. It is likely that this enormous congregation assembled at numerous sites in the city for worship and communion. If that is true, one congregation with one eldership and thousands of members which owned no building did not have a collective assembly. How do these facts fit accepted definitions?

Of further interest is the fact that Titus was left by Paul in Crete to appoint elders in "every city."[17] Could it be that a congregation in the New Testament was all the Christians of a particular city with an eldership overseeing them?

Another Classic Example

Just as with the Pharisees, in the restoration church there are times when traditional authority produced by reasoned conclusions ignore the revealed priorities of the Lord. Jesus' dying prayer for His people was a plea for universal unity, an intercongregational unity. It was to be a genuine unity fashioned after the oneness of the Father and the Son, not a hypothetical unity of mere words. He acknowledged this unity was essential to His goal of converting the world. Without it, the world would have cause for disbelief. That which destroys unity in a congregation or among congregations violates the Lord's priority concern for His people.

Like the Pharisees, many Christians allow reasoned conclusions to void specific revelation. The desire for unity is a revealed, unquestionable priority of the Lord for His people. It is as specific as, "Honor thy father and mother." Yet, human reasoning sanctions divisions among New Testament Christians. That reasoning declares (1) congregational autonomy is sacred and must be preserved. (2) Leadership must be confined to a single congregation. (3) A congregation is a group of Christians meeting in the same building. (4) The autonomy of that group must be preserved regardless of the cost. The conclusion: if division results from preserving autonomy, then division is right and the will of God.

Thus, reasoned conclusions declare that unity can be disregarded, ignored, and even destroyed if the autonomy of a group meeting in a building is threatened. That modern traditional law is as woefully flawed as was the Pharisees' traditional law which set aside the fifth commandment. To build religious practices which ignore revealed divine priorities is to participate in the Pharisees' hypocrisy. As with the Pharisees, such reasoning produces people with hearts removed from the Lord's concerns who honor God with words. Worship becomes vain because "the faith" and "fellowship" are based on human concepts rather than divine revelation.

The Concern

The concern expressed in this chapter is not concern that congregational units of today violate Scripture. There is no specific definition to violate. Substituting one reasoned conclusion for another is hardly an improvement.

The concern expressed is for the effect that modern traditional ordinances are having in setting aside the revealed concerns and objectives of the Lord. This is the plea: (1) for Christians to recognize flaws in their reasoning; (2) for Christians to stop passing judgments on each other on the basis of human reasonings unrelated to revelation; and (3) for Christians to refuse to measure the faithfulness of others by using reasoned conclusions which have little or nothing to do with specific revelation. This is an urgent plea to cease making unity impossible by invoking modern traditional laws which ignore the Lord's prevailing concerns and purposes.

CHAPTER TWELVE
FOOTNOTES

1. *Isaiah 1:18.*
2. *Matthew 26:30.*
3. *Matthew 26:17-19.*
4. *M. Pesahim 10:7.*
5. *Acts 2:42,46,47; 12:5,12; 16:25; 18:12; 20:7.*
6. Everett Ferguson, **Early Christians Speak** *(Sweet Publishing Company: Austin, Texas, 1971), pp. 81-89.*
7. *Acts 8:26-39.*
8. *Acts 14:23; Titus 1:5.*
9. *1 Corinthians 16:1-4; 2 Corinthians 8:1-5; 2 Corinthians 9:1-5; 2 Corinthians 11:8-9.*
10. *Acts 15:4.*
11. *Acts 2:41.*
12. *Acts 2:47.*
13. *Acts 4:4.*
14. *Acts 5:14.*
15. *Acts 6:7.*
16. *Acts 2:46.*
17. *Titus 1:5.*

CHAPTER TWELVE
QUESTIONS

1. In what three ways has it been said that Scripture expresses its authority?
   A. What role does reasoning play in each?
   B. How do subjective determinations create problems in these approaches to defining scriptural authority?
2. Concerning the worship of the Christians of the New Testament:
   A. What is known?
   B. What is not known?

3. By using the invitation song and united assemblies as examples, illustrate the fact that reasoned conclusions can be formulated into unbreakable laws.

4. Why has the concept of congregational autonomy been a vital issue in the restoration movement?
   A. What does Scripture say about intercongregational cooperation in the first century? (Include information from 1 Corinthians 16:1-4 and 2 Corinthians 8:1-5; 9:1-5; and 11:8-9 in your answer.)
   B. Is the same stress concerning congregational autonomy found in the New Testament found in the church today? Why?

5. In the discussion of autonomy, why is the definition of "a congregation" the key definition?
   A. What is the common definition of "a congregation" today?
   B. Based on information in the New Testament, what problems exist in that definition?

6. What priority did Jesus place on the unity of believers?
   A. How do reasoned conclusions set aside that priority?
   B. Show the parallel between the Pharisees' position on, "Honor thy father and mother," and the church's common position on unity today.

7. What is not the author's concern in this chapter?
   A. What is the author's concern?
   B. What is the author's plea?

THOUGHT QUESTION

How can Christians be awakened to the fact that human judgments have been used to make many church laws? How can this be done in a manner which will help unify the church rather than to further divide the church?

CHAPTER THIRTEEN
IN SUMMARY

Another volume could be written easily on expressions of Jewish Pharisaism and their corollaries in present Christian Pharisaism. The expressions of Jewish Pharisaism not dealt with in this writing are numerous. They include the following:

1. Disregarding the spiritual importance of human need
2. Condemning one for uncleanness because of his associations
3. Believing a "righteous end" justifies the means
4. Seeking to destroy a person's godly influence by prejudicial accusation
5. Defending convictions by attacking truth
6. Living by the hypocrisy of external spirituality
7. Living in the blindness which swallows camels and strains gnats
8. Living by the code of self-righteousness

Jewish Pharisaism in a Capsule

Jewish Pharisaism arose in response to living needs and to spiritual questions generated by a changing world. Its spirit was founded in the awareness that the living Word of God had to answer spiritual questions relevantly. The way to preserve the "ancient ways of God" was to apply the intent of Scripture to current needs and questions. This response produced an oral law which sought (1) to interpret the written law, (2) to apply the written law, and (3) to supplement the written law. The oral law existed in respect of and defense of the written law.

The idea and intent was good and necessary. Scripture must be applied accurately to current life if people are to live obediently to its teachings. Scripture's intent must be interpreted accurately if people are to yield to the will of God.

The tragedy of Pharisaism did not lie in a failure to understand the real need. Nor did it lie in an incorrect assessment of that need. The failure of Pharisaism was the result of four things. First, the authority of the oral law at times was substituted for the authority of Scripture. Second, the oral law's interpretations degenerated into a set of rules and regulations to be obeyed mindlessly. Third, at times the oral law misrepresented the intent of Scripture or the priorities of God. Fourth, Pharisaism's objective became to force people to conform to the regulations.

Christian Pharisaism in a Capsule

Christian Pharisaism is a response to living needs and to spiritual questions generated by a changing world. Its spirit is founded in the awareness that the teachings of Christ must answer these questions relevantly. If first-century Christianity is to be restored and preserved, the intent of Scripture must be applied to life's current needs and questions. To meet this challenge, religious positions founded on human judgments declare the intent of New Testament teachings. These positions seek (1) to interpret written Scripture, (2) to apply written Scripture, and (3) to address moral questions not discussed in Scripture, thereby supplementing Scripture. These positions exist in respect of and in defense of written Scripture.

The idea and the intent is good and necessary. If Scripture is to be obeyed by Christians, it must be applied accurately to current life. If Christians are to yield to the will of God, they must interpret the intent of Scripture accurately.

The tragedy of Christian Pharisaism does not lie in a failure to understand a real need. Nor does it lie in an incorrect assessment of the need. The problem created by Christian Pharisaism exists for four reasons. First, there are times when the authority of approved positions is substituted for the authority of Scripture. Second, the declared positions too frequently degenerate into a set of rules and regulations to be followed mindlessly without faith or understanding. Third, at times the positions misrepresent the intent of Scripture or the priorities of Christ. Fourth, too often the objective of those who advocate the positions is to impose conformity to human judgments rather than to generate faith by teaching Scripture.

The Solution

The solution is not to denounce "the system," "the church," or the preaching and leadership of the church. Nothing will be resolved or improved by seeking to start a revolution within the church. To divide again over the use and application of human judgments would not serve the purposes of Christ. The aim of the continuing restoration is correct. The objective is correct. The respect for authority of Scripture is correct. The desire to interpret, to understand, and to apply Scripture is correct. A radical reaction to a real problem would destroy much and solve nothing. The solution is for Christians to accept some responsibilities. They must recognize with honesty areas wherein human judgment is being substituted for Scripture. They must begin building faith on knowledge instead of demanding conformity to regulations. They ceaselessly must study and understand Scripture, and they ceaselessly must be willing to change when they learn and understand. They must recognize human judgments as human judgments, and Scripture as Scripture.

The key to the solution is not another movement in the church. The key is enlightened, understanding individuals. These individuals will substitute understanding for condemnation, listening for confrontation, and respect for arrogance disguised as zeal. These individuals will be believers rather than conformists who mistake conformity for faith. They will live and teach for the purpose of producing more believers. They will not exist to judge the faith of God's family. They will be dedicated to edification, not alienation.

May this study challenge you to become such a Christian individual who wholeheartedly lives for the kingdom of God.

CHAPTER THIRTEEN
QUESTIONS

Recall all that you have learned and understood about Pharisaism. Read the following passages. In each passage or set of passages identify the Pharisaical expression. Discuss how the Pharisaical concept erred. Consider similar problems among Christians today.

1. John 8:1-11
2. Matthew 9:10-13, Luke 5:29-32, Luke 15

3. Matthew 12:14, Luke 11:53-54, John 11:47-53, John 18:3, Matthew 26:59

4. John 9:13-34

5. Matthew 9:32-34, 12:22-27

6. Matthew 23:23-24

7. Matthew 23:25-28

8. Luke 18:9-14